MW01033522

Praise for Entrusted

"*Entrusted* is truly remarkable. It is very well written, easy to follow and compelling. I believe it will assist many families in dealing with their heritage and what they hope their lives can produce."

Jonathan Blattmachr
Esq., Principal, Interactive Legal

"It is rare to find a book that challenges the status quo, while at the same time, offers unique and inspiring alternatives to the age-old tradition of traditional estate planning. David York and Andrew Howell, prominent estate planning attorneys, are fed up with the traditional, sterile, tax driven approach to estate planning. With years of experience and researching successful multi-generational families, they not only share "Why" there is a revolution afoot to change how estate planning is done; they also present encouraging solutions that support active living legacies that will outlive you through the generations. If you love your family and desire to have a lasting impact, then *Entrusted* is a must read."

Lee Brower
Author, *The Brower Quadrant*

"The concepts in *Entrusted* are critically important to change the destiny for many families and to avoid raising children consumed with entitlement. York and Howell feel more like great writers than merely attorneys as the issues discussed in this book are profound and are articulated with ease and explained with such simplicity that it is magic. It is the blueprint for holistic wealth transfer."

Garrett Gunderson
Author, *Killing Sacred Cows*

"I am asked to read a lot of books each regarding planning around finances. When I picked up *Entrusted,* I thought that it was going to be the same information I had heard time and time before. However, I began reading it and immediately fell in love with the message. It kept me reading and engaged until I reached the very last page."

Jon Butcher
CEO, Precious Moments
and Founder, LifeBook

"*Entrusted* is powerful and insightful! The authors were able to take a difficult and sometimes boring subject and transform it into a compelling read. I will definitely be recommending this book to all of my clients."

Cathy Angstman
Vice President and Senior Fiduciary
Advisory Specialist, Wells Fargo Private Bank

"What a timely, comprehensive and insightful effort! So few are the families that have, or may obtain, enough experience, resources and wisdom to garner into focus the very things so artfully outlined in *Entrusted*. Any family interested in *substantive* family purpose would find this book to be of immense value."

Paul M. Jensen
Founder, PMJ Companies

"To be honest, I was not expecting to enjoy this book as much as I had anticipated, but wow, I ate up every word! I plan on getting *Entrusted* into the hands of every one of my clients."

Marc Simmons
CPA, Simmons & Company

ENTRUSTED

ENTRUSTED

BUILDING A LEGACY THAT LASTS

DAVID R. YORK | ANDREW L. HOWELL

Published by:
YH Publishing, LLC
6405 South 3000 East, Suite 150
Salt Lake City, Utah 84121
info@entrustedplanning.com

Printed in the United States of America

ISBN Hardcover: 978-0-692-55826-3
ISBN eBook: 978-0-692-55827-0

Library of Congress Control Number: 2015955219

Cover Design: YH Publishing, LLC
Interior Design: Ghislain Viau

This is dedicated to our wives, Mindy and Candice and our children, Emma, John, Samuel, Hudson, Avery, Thomas, Harrison and Madeline. You are our greatest legacies.

Table of Contents

Introduction

If you want to build a ship, don't drum up people to collect wood, and don't assign them tasks and work, but rather teach them to long for the endless immensity of the sea.
—Antoine de Saint-Exupéry

THERE ARE TWO PRIMARY REASONS we decided to write this book. The first is to bring to the fore that wealth is far more than numbers on a balance sheet. The transfer of your wealth *in all its forms* is and should be your primary objective when it comes to your estate planning. As each of us gets older and collects more life experience, we begin to realize that wealth has many meanings and touches virtually all aspects of our lives. Our health, education, life experiences, family, friends, personal and business relationships, physical fitness, spiritual beliefs, and overall quality of life are all aspects of our lives that can and should be viewed as markers of *wealth*.

Our ancestors had this broader view of wealth and saw the holistic transfer of wealth as one of their primary responsibilities in life. The reality is that easily transferrable and highly liquid assets are a relatively recent phenomenon. Wealth transfer prior to The Industrial Revolution and the creation of capital markets was primarily about two things: the transfer of intellectual wealth (in the form of knowledge, wisdom, abilities, and experience) and the transfer of opportunities (in the form of tools, resources, and land). It's time to get back to the roots of wealth transfer and to focus on the transfer of wealth in the broadest sense of the term.

Although we intuitively know that wealth is far more than dollars in the bank, when it comes to estate planning and the effective transfer of that wealth, most discussions involving the terms *wealth* and *money* use those terms interchangeably. Although the two are not the same, most of our colleagues in the estate planning community do not even broach this concept with their clients or include the less tangible aspects of wealth as they draft an estate plan. They simply develop a plan that prepares the family's financial assets to be dumped, divided, deferred, and dissipated among the members of the next generation.

These estate plans also reflect a very linear way of thinking. In other words, if transferring some amount of financial wealth is good, then transferring more financial wealth is better. Not only do we think this approach is myopic and simplistic, we also think it's ultimately destructive because it focuses on the fire (the result) and not on the flint and kindling (the tools and resources that produce the result).

The second reason we wrote this book is to help you understand that money is a tool, nothing more or less, and that the point of a tool is to use it to *do* something and not just to *be* something. Merriam-Webster defines the word "tool" in its noun form as follows: "something (as an instrument or apparatus) used in performing an operation or necessary in the practice of a vocation or profession." Based on this definition, isn't money one of the most versatile tools of all?

The reality is that money is in itself neither good nor evil. Although money has no personality or human characteristics, it is often portrayed in a negative light. While money is a versatile tool, as it grows it becomes more and more powerful and, like all powerful tools, shouldn't be handed over to someone unprepared for how to use it. Yet, far too many people ignore this reality when it comes to their children—leaving them, for good or for ill, to learn that lesson on their own.

In our estate planning practices, we are witnessing a fundamental shift in how generations view the passage of wealth. Many of our clients have seen first hand the destructive potential of unharnessed and undirected inheritances. Most people blame *the money* when unprepared heirs act in ways that are not only outside of the realm of what any reasonable person would consider commendable but also ultimately self-destructive.

This concern causes many very financially successful individuals to take the position that other wealthy individuals have taken: "We're going to give all the money to charity so as not to create trust fund babies. They didn't earn the money and therefore won't value it. I'm afraid that it will harm or even destroy their motivation to succeed."

The sentiment behind this statement, of course, is a good one. It's like a derivative of the Hippocratic oath applied to estate planning: *Primum non nocere* (First, do no harm). Ideally, everyone finds something that they are passionate about and that gives them a sense of purpose and direction when they rise every morning. They should become a productive member of society and be financially self-sufficient.

Giving all of your assets to a charitable organization so as to avoid spoiling your children and to encourage their self-sufficiency is an understandable response. However, to a large extent this thinking is no different than dumping all the assets on your children without the proper preparation. The charity didn't earn the money, either. You simply end up shifting the stewardship of your financial resources to a charity and bypassing the important process of financially educating and preparing your family. The crisis may have been averted, but the opportunity held within it has been lost.

Your child's school will not teach them about finances. That's up to you. In divesting your financial wealth, you also preclude the ability to access resources in the case of an unforeseen emergency incurred by one of your loved ones.

Although charitable giving is commendable and should be an important part of any high-net-worth person's planning, it should be no more than one aspect of the plan and not the full plan.

As you read this book, ask yourself the following questions: What were you taught by your parents about wealth? Did money equal wealth in your household, or was wealth something more? Was the entire subject of money taboo and therefore not discussed at all? What have you taught your family about who you are as a collective group and the impact your intimate group will have on humanity? How do you hope or plan to transfer wealth to successive generations? And, perhaps most important, do you have a vision for your wealth?

We hope this book will be an awakening for you about different ways to think of the concept of wealth and its transfer through generations. We hope this book, if it does nothing else, will cause you to raise the questions with your own family and certainly with the professional planners assisting you with these matters.

This book is a compilation of what we've experienced in our nearly fifty years collectively dealing with high-net-worth individuals, plus some case studies of other well-known, prominent figures throughout history. We consider them *best practices* for those truly interested in holistic wealth transfer. The disciplines laid out in this book are the common threads among those families that have been able to truly build legacies that last.

We realize that there are many books out there that address some of these concepts. Unfortunately, many of those books fall into one of two very distinct categories. First, there are books that are highly inspiring or motivational, but ultimately don't provide any meaningful or concrete suggestions for implementation. The other category comprises the legal treatises, in which technical and legal concepts are presented in depth; but for the reader without legal training, they become nothing more than a nighttime sleep aid.

Our hope is to convey the best of these two extremes so that you are empowered to take charge of your family's future and come away with the tools and processes necessary to fashion an estate plan that captures the heart, soul, and vision of your family and your wealth.

A Word about Family

Throughout this book, we use the term *family*. We realize that there are many successful individuals and couples who don't have children but who still desire to make a meaningful and positive multigenerational impact in the world. If you're one of those people, realize that the term *family* has a broad definition that can include extended families, close friends, employees, affinity groups, religious bodies, and even entire communities. In fact, there are certain types of trusts that can be established today and that can operate not for specific individuals but for specific purposes, like advancing education, continuing to operate a business, or supporting and benefiting a specific community.

However you define family and whatever family you choose, we hope this book will speak directly to your needs and inspire you to be purposeful and intentional in implementing your planning and transferring the whole of your wealth.

Chapter 1

Estate Planning Today and Why It's Broken

What you leave behind is not what is engraved in stone monuments, but what is woven into the lives of others.
—Pericles

What's It Worth?

THERE ONCE WAS A WEALTHY father who ran several very successful businesses. His only son was the heir apparent, but the father was worried about his son's lack of work ethic. One day, the father called his son into his office and said, "I will set up my affairs so that you will ultimately inherit all my businesses, but first, I want you to go out and earn $10,000 on your own and bring it to me."

The son agreed, but instead of going out and earning the money, he went to his father's banker with a tempting proposition. "If you loan me the $10,000 my father has asked me to earn," he said to the banker, "I'll repay you with high interest when I take over his many businesses."

The banker agreed and six months later, the son went to his father and presented his father with the money. The father took the money, walked across the room, and threw it in the fireplace. "You didn't earn that money," the father said. "Go back out into the world, earn $10,000, and then I'll set up my affairs so that you ultimately inherit all my businesses."

The son figured the banker must have told his father about their deal, so this time around he decided to make the same proposition, but to a friend who lived in another town. "If you loan me $10,000 and tell no one, I'll repay you double when I take over my father's businesses."

The friend knew a good deal when he saw one and agreed. Again, six months later, the son went to his father and presented the money. Again, the father took the money, threw it in the fireplace, and said, "You didn't earn that money. Go out, earn $10,000, and then I'll set up my affairs so that you ultimately inherit all my businesses."

The son was bewildered. *How did my father know I hadn't earned the money?* Realizing that it would likely be impossible to ever fool his father, the son knew he had no choice but to earn the money himself. Begrudgingly, he went out and took on every job he could find, working day and night. Once he had accumulated $10,000, he confidently and proudly went to his father to present the money, only to be shocked when his father *again* threw the money in the fireplace!

The son, without thinking, dove toward the fireplace and immediately started pulling out the cash and beating out the flames.

"Now," the father said, "I know that you earned that money."

For the most part, something is worth what it costs you. If you bought two paintings, one on the street for two dollars and one from an art gallery for $200,000, you'll probably roll up the two dollar painting and take it with you, but perhaps not with the greatest level of care. The $200,000 painting, on the other hand, would likely be wrapped by professionals and delivered to your door, where you'd sign for it personally and then insure and secure it.

When you work and sacrifice to acquire something, it has greater value to you than something that's simply given to you. This is also true when it comes to inheritance. The sad reality is that outright transfer of assets to heirs is usually accompanied with a diminished value being placed on those assets because they've cost those heirs little or nothing.

An Age-Old Concern

Concern about the negative effects of unearned wealth transfer is not new. In the western world, we're quite familiar with stories of inheritance gone wrong. In Dickens's *Great Expectations*, Pip squanders his family's money and lands on the debauched streets of England. In *Citizen Kane*, Charles Foster Kane's life is shaped by his parents' inheritance of a gold mine.

In the early eighteenth century, English artist William Hogarth painted a series of eight paintings known as *A Rake's Progress*, in which we see Tom Rakewell's descent from fortunate heir into, literally, Bedlam (the most infamous mental asylum in history). In the first painting, shortly after receiving his inheritance, Tom is seen rejecting his pregnant fiancé's hand while having new clothes tailored to fit him. In the next painting, fancy friends and admirers surround him, but by the third painting (see image below), he is a drunk gallivanting in a brothel. By the seventh painting, not long after marrying an "ugly old hag" for her riches and then gambling them away, Tom is in debtor's prison. His prison cellmate is writing a pamphlet on how to solve the national debt crisis. Finally, Tom ends up insane and institutionalized.

In the New Testament, Jesus tells the story of the prodigal son, in which a young son is so desperate for a share of his father's wealth that he simply cannot wait to inherit it. He begs for the money, receives it, and, of course, wastes it all. Caught in a famine that sweeps the land, the son is reduced to herding pigs—the lowliest of all jobs at the time. He is saved from his plight only when he returns home and casts himself on the mercy of his father.

The Reformation Movement

The history of estate planning in Western civilization can be divided into three separate and distinct phases. In the first phase, which began in roughly 1200 AD and lasted until the start of the industrial revolution in about 1760 AD, estate planning was primarily focused on the transfer of land and titles of nobility. In fact, the genesis of trust law comes from land ownership and succession planning for the continued ownership and management of property, within multiple generations of the same family line, usually to the eldest male.

The transfer of land and titles of nobility was, however, simply the transfer of opportunity from one generation to the next, and in essence, was the transfer of a means to an end. Plans and contingencies had to be developed to properly and effectively transfer the land to the next generation and significant foresight was put into plans for the control and management of the land. Descendants still had to work, protect, and preserve the land. Heirs had to have faith that crops wouldn't be destroyed by natural disaster or man-made factors.

Trust law was first developed during the Crusades. A nobleman heading off on a quest had no idea if he would return or not, so he would entrust his land in the name of someone who would oversee and manage it for the benefit of his family—until his return.

Problems arose when some of these noblemen arrived home. The people they had entrusted with their land were unwilling to return it. They had grown accustomed to the opportunities and wealth that the land provided. This problem became common enough that over time the courts of that day developed the concept of a trust, in which you gave an asset to a person to hold for the benefit of yourself or others. After so many "trusts built on handshakes" went wrong, trusting your estate—in life and upon death—became focused not just on *what* was entrusted, but on the *who and how*.

Trust law during this time was built with a focus on the character and fitness of the parties involved. *The relationship between the parties involved came before the question of assets.* When setting up a trust, the first and most important decision was not about the assets of the trust or even the ultimate beneficiaries. Trusts were first about the trustee—the person placed in charge of the assets of the trust. The term *trust* literally related to *trusting* someone with assets for the benefit of someone else. It focused on the character, fitness, and ability of the person *trusted* with the assets to care for the beneficiaries. Trusts were first about relationship, character, and ability before they were ever about the assets.

The second phase of wealth transfer in Western civilization began with the Industrial Revolution and the creation of capital markets. Wealth became decoupled from land and began to be accumulated in more liquid assets such as cash, stock, bonds, and other intangible assets. Accordingly, estate planning and wealth transfer became increasingly focused on the *end* rather than on the *means to the end,* and recipients of that more liquid wealth had immediate enjoyment.

As a result, people began to see the negative effects of inherited wealth manifested in so-called "trust fund babies," "trustfunders," or "trustafarians," a play on the word "Rastafarian." In the twenty-first century, the term *affluenza*—an influenza of affluence—emerged to describe those circumstances in which wealth, particularly inherited wealth, can all too often cause financial illness and disease.

In fact, in 2013 affluenza even became a legal defense in a Texas courtroom in the case of Ethan Couch, a young man who had killed four people while driving under the influence of drugs. In that case, a psychologist who testified in the trial argued that Ethan suffered from affluenza, and as a result he couldn't appreciate the fact his activities had consequences because he had been taught that wealth buys privilege.[1]

The third phase of wealth transfer is what's happening in estate planning today. Having witnessed the negative effects of highly liquid inherited wealth in friends and family, many wealth creators are looking for alternatives, and some are shifting back to the original roots of modern wealth transfer. Today, people are increasingly interested in structuring their

---

1 Neil, Marta (2/6/14) "Affluenza teen on Probation for for fatal crash is sent to pricey rehab." American Bar Association.

plan to encourage and support the behaviors, values, and characteristics they cherish, with the hope and expectation that by focusing their wealth, it will in turn encourage successive generations to accumulate their own wealth and receive with it an accompanying sense of accomplishment.

This shift in how people see estate planning and wealth transfer is not merely anecdotal. According to a recent study conducted by U.S. Trust[2], roughly 77 percent of the Silent Generation (those born between 1925 and 1945), consider wealth transfer very important, and 21 percent of that same generation believe they are obligated to transfer wealth to the next generation. Compare that with the results of that same study which shows that less than half of Baby Boomers (those born between 1946 and 1964) think wealth transfer is important, and that only 3 percent of them believe they have any obligation to leave their children anything. These numbers represent a huge and ongoing shift that continues to widen with successive generations.

In the context of wealth transfer and estate planning, we sit at a particularly interesting juncture in time. The Silent Generation is currently in the process of transferring $12 trillion to their heirs. The Baby Boomers, on the other hand, are poised to pass over $40 trillion to the next generation.[3] It will represent the largest financial wealth transfer in the history of

2 *U.S. Trust Survey – Insights on Wealth and Worth and Allianz American Legacies Pulse Survey*
3 Accenture, The "Greater" Wealth Transfer: Capitalizing on the Intergenerational Shift in Wealth, 2012.

the world. This massive and unprecedented transfer, combined with the general dissatisfaction in the past few years regarding traditional estate planning, has led to the perfect storm. We're witnessing the greatest transfer of financial wealth in human history—and yet there is widespread confusion and disillusionment on how best to implement the transfer.

The Lady or the Tiger?

Alfred Nobel (see Case Study, Page 44) was a nineteenth century chemist and inventor. His most famous invention was dynamite, a stable form of otherwise highly unstable liquid nitroglycerin. Dynamite—its name derived from the Greek word *dynamos*, meaning power—was used to build tunnels more safely, mine natural resources, and fuel economic development. Dynamite was also used to create more powerful and effective landmines, bombs, and weaponry. It was a tool for good and for destruction.

Financial wealth is like dynamite in at least three ways:

1. It can be used for good or for evil.
2. The more there is, the more of an impact it will make.
3. The ultimate question is never "Will it have an impact?" but rather "What *kind* of impact will it have?"

Many individuals approach financial wealth transfer with caution and perhaps even trepidation over the potential negative effects that the transfer of their assets at death could have on successive generations. Instead of confidently passing resources to the next generation to steward, grow, and fully use their wealth, too many parents cringe at the thought of the potential for destruction that such a transfer will have on their children. They feel as though they're handing over financial dynamite that could cause untold destruction to their future generations. The concerns grow larger still in situations where a child may already have a personal issue, such as a substance abuse problem, which would certainly be exacerbated by having significant assets available.

All too often, those concerned about the potential negative impact inherited wealth will have on their children or family members feel as though they have only one of two options: to dump it on their successors or to give it away to somebody else.

The standard model for most modern estate plans is to dump, divide, defer, and dissipate. This model involves *dumping* the assets to the next generation, *dividing* them among the children, attempting to *defer* any taxes, and finally *dissipating* those assets within one or two generations at most. It's a shotgun approach to wealth transfer. It's like building a roaring campfire, then trying to divide up the burning logs among all the people huddled around and expecting them to effectively care for, transport, and replicate that fire. It's largely because of the dump, divide, defer, and dissipate model of estate planning that 90 percent of wealth accumulated by the first generation is gone by the third.[4]

---

4 CNN Money. "Squandering the family fortune: Why rich families are losing money." June 25, 2014. http://money.cnn.com/2014/06/25/luxury/family-wealth/

Very often, individuals who default into the modern estate planning model, usually due to the ignorance of any other way, will attempt to mitigate the potential negative effects of this model by engaging in the strategy that we call *hiding the ball*. Essentially, they keep as much financial information from their children or heirs as possible in an attempt to reduce the likelihood that they will develop the dreaded feeling of entitlement. Although the children may have some inkling of their parents' net worth based on their lifestyle, they're given no real or meaningful information on what their parents are worth, how the parents or family made their money, or what to expect if their parents die. The hope is that, without feelings of entitlement developing, they will seek to become self-sufficient, but hiding the ball often garners mixed results, at best.

The second option is *giving it all away*. Parents who choose this option also have little concern for financial assistance to their children beyond acquiring a house or starting a business. The remaining assets at death are directed to one or more various charitable organizations. This strategy has become quite popular and its followers include highly respected entrepreneurs, business leaders, and entertainers. Warren Buffett has committed 90 percent of his $72 billion to the Bill and Melinda Gates Foundation, itself the beneficiary of a $40 billion gift from the founder of Microsoft himself, Bill Gates. He has publically stated that his children will receive "only a miniscule" proportion of his wealth because he wants them to build their own fortunes—if fortune is what they want—by finding jobs they love and working hard at them.[5]

Kevin O'Leary, Mr. Wonderful on ABC's *Shark Tank*, has taken a similar tack. He has said that although he will absorb the full cost of his children's educational expenses, they will not receive one penny of his $300 million net worth after his death. For O'Leary, it's crucial that his son and daughter learn to make their own way in the world. Likewise, successful musician Sting has referred to trust funds as "albatrosses 'round [children's] necks," and Nigella Lawson has said, "I'm determined that my children should have no financial security. Not having to earn money ruins people."[6]

Although charitable intent is often an important component of this decision, so too is the desire to avoid giving children too much, since they didn't earn the money and, therefore, will likely not value it and may even waste it. It's often more about where the money *isn't* going (to their family) than where it *is* going (to charity). The irony of this choice is that the funds are given to an organization that likewise didn't earn it and may potentially end up stewarding it as poorly or more poorly than the children would have. Charitable organizations are sometimes inefficient, and well-intentioned altruism is instead used for the high

5 Kirkland, Jr., Richard. "Fortune." Should You Leave It All to the Children? September 29, 1986. Accessed October 28, 2015.

6 Roberts, Roxanne. *Washington Post, Why the Super Rich Aren't Leaving Much of their Fortunes to their Kids*, August 10, 2014.

administrative costs of running the charity. Did the donor intend his life's work to pay for these ancillary items?

A Third Door

Although it's important to make sure that you carefully and thoughtfully share financial information in age-appropriate ways, and although charitable giving is and should be an important part of any plan, the fundamental question is this: *Why should you ultimately deploy your assets at death in a way that you never would have while you were alive?* In other words, why shouldn't your estate plan and your dealings with your children, heirs, and society align with your goals, values, and beliefs? What if, instead of dumping, dividing, and dissipating assets, you focused on transferring wisdom and opportunity and fostered self-reliance, sustainability, and productivity?

Entrusted Planning

Entrusted Planning is the process of aligning the principles and values of a family with their tangible assets and structures and prepares future generations to build a true and lasting legacy. It's a process that draws from the very origins of estate law, which placed the highest value on *who* was involved—on who was entrusted. Entrusted Planning goes back to preparing beneficiaries for wealth beyond just the legal concept of a trust and takes into account the relational maturation of the person or persons being entrusted as *stewards* of resources, not just consumers and users of it.

Entrusted Planning is about transferring opportunities instead of just assets and doing so over multiple generations. It's as much about being as generous and optimistic with future generations as it is about being generous with charity.

The concepts behind Entrusted Planning can be seen as far back as some five thousand years ago. The Talmud teaches that parents must raise their children, teach them the Torah (God's word), a trade, and it even instructs parents to teach their children how to swim. In other words, it teaches each of us that our primary responsibility to our children is to give them the tools they'll need to know who they are and how to be self-sufficient in the world. By focusing on the means to an end (education, personal character, home ownership, entrepreneurship, charitable service) as opposed to the end (stocks, bonds, real estate, and businesses), Entrusted Planning has the greatest potential to do the maximum amount of multigenerational good with the least amount of collateral damage.

Modern Estate Planning versus Entrusted Planning

Modern Estate Planning

Modern estate planning is *asset-focused* and usually does not take into account the individuals, personalities, and unique dynamics of each family. It's based on a *linear* way of thinking; that is, if transferring some wealth is good, it follows that transferring more wealth is better.

Modern estate planning tends to be *tool-driven,* which leads most planners to jump to strategies that pass along economic capital without taking into account the individual's or family's human capital. Not taking human capital into consideration when planning the transfer of wealth would be like asking a contractor to build your vacation home, only to have him tell you how many 2x4s will be needed, how many shingles, and how many windows. It makes no sense to start building something without first knowing what you are building and *why.*

In addition to being asset-focused, linear, and tool-driven, modern estate planning is *generic.* Many estate plans are written in third person, with the only personal information being an inclusion of the person's name and sometimes the names of their children. They tend to be focused exclusively on financial assets and taxes. Estate planning software has only increased this generic nature of planning. The idea that a person can do his or her own estate planning is tantamount to someone attempting to perform their own root canal.

Finally, because many people have learned to think of estate planning as a transaction rather than a relationship, they believe their estate plans are done. And yet, most of us would never say that our family is done. We're constantly and consistently trying to educate and empower our family members. Families are constantly growing, learning, adapting, and developing, as is the ever-changing tax code. Estate planning should reflect that state of continual evolution, but modern estate planning all too often remains *static.*

Our experience has shown that even when an estate plan is in place, it usually hasn't been reviewed in at least ten to fifteen years. The problem with this static model is that there is no room for it to adapt and evolve into new and better paradigms. All estate plans, whether entrusted or not, should be reviewed and updated regularly.

Entrusted Planning

Entrusted Planning differs from modern estate planning first in that it is *beneficiary-focused*. Entrusted Planning is more about preparing future generations to maximize their potential than it is about transferring wealth for the sake of the wealth. It focuses on what is needed for this to be accomplished.

Entrusted Planning is based on *specific goals, values,* and *beliefs*—those that are ongoing and everlasting and those that have more recently percolated to the surface. A multigenerational wealth plan cannot be built on outdated assumptions. Before any lasting plan can be implemented, it's critical to first identify the values, vision, and mission of the particular family, in their particular time and setting.

Entrusted Planning is *purpose-driven*—trusts, limited liability companies, charitable strategies, and other wealth-transfer devices are seen as nothing more than tools to accomplish the family's goals. Knowing the goal is the only way to have foresight to know when and how to use the tools.

Doing away with the generic, Entrusted Planning is *customized*. It recognizes that families are unique, and their planning should also be unique. An Entrusted Plan is custom built and takes into account the specific situations, people, and resources that make up each family and its wealth.

Finally, because a family[7] is never *done*, an Entrusted Plan *includes regular maintenance and updating* to stay relevant and effective. Imagine paying someone to come in and design an award-winning backyard, put it in place, and declare it done. It wouldn't take long for weeds to overtake it. An Entrusted Plan may be up to date for any given period of time, but it's never completed. This means an effective Entrusted Plan should be consistently reviewed and updated as new family members enter the picture, people age, desires change, and Congress changes tax laws.

It's important to note that many of the tools of modern estate planning serve important functions. Financial and medical powers of attorney, wills, and revocable living trusts are critical tools that every adult should thoughtfully implement. We call this foundational planning, and it's critical to effectively provide for individuals and families in the event of disability or death. Regardless of the size of a person's estate, this foundational planning is vital. In fact, for most families, foundational estate planning is all that's needed from a legal standpoint and can effectively work in conjunction with the implementation of the disciplines outlined in this book.

---

7 Recall that, as we discussed in the introduction, family can and should have broad definition.

That said, the one-size-fits-all mentality of modern estate planning could cause disastrous results as you travel along the wealth continuum. Many professional planners are either unaware of the possibilities or uninterested in assisting their clients in developing a truly tailored and personal plan. Instead, they focus on the volume of clients, thus turning their practices into *trust mills*.

Transferring Wealth with Grace

In old movies, the *reading of the will* scene is always the same: The executor sits behind a heavy ornate desk and calls out each child by name, stating how much he or she is to inherit. Usually, someone is slighted, tempers flare, and high drama ensues. Unfortunately, not much has changed.

Your wealth is one of the most personal things you'll transfer, so why would you want it to do in death what you would never have wanted it to do while you were living? In other words, you might tell your children as they're heading off to college: "You can go do anything, but you can't do nothing." And yet what does your estate plan say? If it's based on a traditional model, it probably says, "If I die, here's a whole wad of money. Go do whatever you want with it."

This kind of disconnect is what Entrusted Planning seeks to fix. You value your children being active contributors to society while you are living, and you certainly hope for nothing less after you're gone. All things considered, including the issue of scale, you have to ask yourself, "What would I leave to my family members right now that would be enough to protect them, but not so much as to completely disrupt their lives by causing them to lose the motivation to produce? How can I return to the roots of estate planning and trust law, which were to build on the ability and character of the recipient and to focus on a legacy of opportunities, as opposed to just assets alone?"

For the children of high-net-worth clients, the inheritance of their parents' wealth will be the single most seminal event of their lives. Though the general public might balk at the idea, the truth is that for most wealthy families, inheritance can become a negative and even destructive experience.

In modern estate planning, somebody passes away and the family is instantly thrown into chaos. Sides are drawn, and money is thrown at lawyers in order to *keep* more money. Like dynamite being handed to the unskilled and unprepared, instead of being handled safely and responsibly, the financial wealth blows up in everyone's faces due to a lack of preparedness—and all at a time where there is normally already a sense of loss.

The Entrusted Planning process, by contrast, empowers those with the desire to harness and guide positive growth and change through their descendants. Our clients do not hide the dynamite; they prepare their children to inherit wealth, as well as the opportunities that should come with it. Entrusted Planning begins to unfold well before "the reading of the will" and Entrusted Planning beneficiaries are not surprised by the plan, they are prepared for it.

Entrusted Planning sees the family as a team—one that's responsible for helping, educating, and communicating with each other. Entrusted Planning seeks to align everyone, across the generations, to create a mentality and a set of meaningful goals that, in addition to the financial assets, will be shared and passed along graciously.

The Seven Disciplines of Entrusted Planning

Entrusted Planning is built on seven disciplines which can be found across a multitude of successful high-net-worth families going back hundreds of years. These are not hypothetical or idealistic disciplines. These disciplines are real, and they permeate through the families who have embraced these concepts.

1. Entrusted families know who they are and what they believe.
2. Entrusted families prepare the family for the wealth and not just the financial wealth for the family.
3. Entrusted families maximize the positive benefits of the financial wealth and minimize the negative effects.
4. Entrusted families focus on flint and kindling and not on the fire.
5. Entrusted families are generous.
6. Entrusted families preserve and protect wealth.

7. Entrusted families design and implement dynamic governance.

When you get to the point at which you're putting your wealth behind a statement such as "We are the Smiths. This is what we believe in, this is what we value, and this is what we do to impact the world," you're already well ahead of the game. Entrusted Planning intends to get you to this point and beyond. This is the ultimate goal. You're not simply preparing your beneficiaries for a transfer of financial wealth. You're preparing them to carry on the family's values, philanthropic commitments, and larger goals, all of which are embodied by the seven disciplines.

The successful men and women we work with have goals that are both deep and broad. They're less interested in preparing their families to be *rich* and more interested in preparing them to manage, sustain, and carry on a *rich legacy*—the same legacy they have been building their entire lives.

QUESTIONS TO CONSIDER

1. Does the concept of money transfer being like the transfer of dynamite resonate with you? Why or why not?

2. What obligations, if any, do you feel to successive generations?

3. Have you seen successful wealth transfer occur in your life? Unsuccessful? What elements were present that you felt influenced the success or failure?

4. Are you worried about the effect that inherited wealth will have on your family's future generations?

5. Does your current estate plan even remotely reflect who you are as a person?

Chapter 2

Discipline 1:
Entrusted Families Know Who
They Are and What They Believe

*"Tell me and I forget, teach me and
I may remember. Involve me and I learn."*
—Benjamin Franklin

"WHO AM I? WHY AM I here?" In 1992, Admiral James Stockdale, running mate of Ross Perot, opened the vice presidential debate with those questions. Although he attempted to proceed to answer them, it was too late. The crowd laughed, the media had a field day, and they branded Stockdale as clueless. His opening statement went down as one of the worst quotes in modern United States political history. Although not the best opening for a debate, the questions of who you are and why you're here are fundamental to an understanding of Entrusted Planning.

When you can answer those questions as a family and identify your core values, you create a sense of commonality, and encourage connection. Most families could guess what drives them and makes them unique; they just don't know how to adequately express it. Being able to articulate who you are and why you're here is critical in three respects. The first is that it will create a greater sense of unity among the family members. The second is that it will drive your estate planning and align the use of your financial assets with your principles and values. Third, clearly articulated values will help your professional advisors align those values with your financial resources.

When there is a lack of alignment between values and assets, traditional estate planning strays the farthest afield and does the most damage to relationships and people. For example, for many of our clients, a guiding value of their family is self-reliance, and yet the estate plan they have in place when we first meet too often says, "If I die, here's a whole bunch of money, go do anything you want with it." That lack of direction and guidance is completely inconsistent with their value of self-reliance. Entrusted Planning seeks to connect the dots between the principles and values of the family and the use of assets.

Entrusted Planning also recognizes that the most valuable asset in your family is the human capital of all family members. If an uncle you respected passed away and left you both a personal letter and a list of the assets he left you, which of those would you open first? The letter contains the wisdom and represents the relationship. The assets he accumulated merely flowed from that wisdom and experience.

Human capital encompasses your history, good and bad, your reputation, your core values, life lessons, education (both formal and informal), and your relationships. It's your collective life experience as well as how your beliefs and values were formed. It's your successes and failures and all the intangible tools you've relied on to become who you are today.

Principles, Values, Lessons, and Preferences

The first discipline of Entrusted Planning starts by identifying the *guiding principles, core values, life lessons,* and *personal preferences* of your family. For some, these terms seem interchangeable, but an understanding of the uniqueness and differences between them can allow you to harness their power and use them to effectively guide your family, your vision, and your planning.

Guiding principles are transcendent truths or beliefs that govern and dictate *why* we do what we do. They include our ethics, morals, and views of right and wrong. The word "principle" is derived from the Latin *principium*, meaning source, origin, or beginning. Guiding principles tend to exist whether we acknowledge them or not, but identifying them helps us identify our values and make better decisions. They can often be expressed as statements of fact. Some examples of guiding principles include:

- The more humble you are, the more likely you are to learn and the less likely you are to run into conflict. When you realize that you don't know everything and that everyone on this planet has something that they can teach you, you will have opportunities and experiences that will far outweigh any traditional education.
- The happiest people are typically those who are most grateful.
- Forgiveness is an act that frees both the offender and the offended.
- Those who live with integrity and character will reap long-term benefits.
- It is through sacrifice that we show both value and respect.

Core values are those ideals that we esteem, seek after, and cherish. They are *what* we do and what drive us to action. The word *value* comes from the Latin word for strength, and it originally meant material worth. Over time, it came to mean innate worth. You can also think of it as being synonymous with lifestyle priorities. Although most individuals and groups see the merit in most values, there are certain specific core values that tend to drive one individual or group more than others.

Examples of core values include:[1]

Artistic Values

Artistry: Creative skill to take endeavors to a higher, more expressive level

---

1 List of terms reprinted courtesy of Rivets, the Game, LLC™

Beauty: More than superficial, the qualities that give pleasure to the senses or meaning for the heart, an intense
pleasure or deep satisfaction

Compassion: Sympathetic concern for others' distress and
a desire to alleviate it, taking action to alleviate the
suffering of others

Connection: Relating to others on a deeper level where lasting
bonds are made and meaningful community is created

Creativity: A perspective of openness to new approaches
and their application in inventing and making new ideas
or things

Excellence: Striving for a high standard of quality even when
more effort is required, refusal to settle for mediocrity
in one's endeavors

Experience: First-hand interaction with a subject, and valuing
the accumulation of this experience over years

Humor: An ability to laugh at unexpected life moments,
joking as a way of relating to others and building bonds,
finding joy in the lighter side of things

Ingenuity: Clever in inventing new ideas, resourceful in
finding solutions

Optimism: Seeing the positive in situations and people
even when faced with much negativity, a perspective
of focusing on and celebrating the good parts of life,
a persistent hope and faith in things being better soon

Uniqueness: Valuing originality, the essence of being
singular in a crowd of similar, and making differences
for this purpose

Productive Values

Achievement: Reaching goals by working hard, measuring value by accomplishment, not just effort

Determination: Striving for something despite challenges, persisting in efforts towards a goal in the face of difficulties

Entrepreneurism: The leadership, energy, and devotion to initiate new business enterprises

Health: Physical condition that enables the activities of a fulfilling life and the mental state to appreciate and enjoy it

Independence: Self-reliance that empowers one to determine their own direction, a freedom from reliance on other people and requirements

Knowledge: Learning from experience and education that empowers one to practice and understand things

Leadership: A power of personality and relationships to guide others and motivate them to follow

Productivity: Efficiency of a person in creating and accomplishing, a great amount of achievement, fast progress

Recognition: Acknowledgment by others of one's skills, abilities, or achievements, public or personally stated accolades or rewards

Self-Control: Containing one's own emotions, desires, and behavior in pursuit of a greater purpose, especially in difficult situations

Strength: Endurance of one's spirit through trials, inner fortitude to overcome obstacles and progress towards goals

Ethical Values

Accountability: Owning the consequences of one's actions

Forgiveness: Release of anger that was directed at someone, acceptance of someone in spite of their wrong

Honesty: Communicating truthfully even when it would be easier or beneficial not to

Honor: A respect from others earned through noble acts

Humility: Thinking more of others than one's self

Integrity: Staying true to something when faced with pressure to deviate

Justice: Fairness, equality, ownership of consequences by those responsible for them

Loyalty: Commitment to a person or plan for the long term and through trials

Respect: A show of importance and worth of one's self or others

Responsibility: Taking complete personal ownership over the well-being of something or someone, accepting the full good or bad consequences of one's choices and actions

Sacrifice: Giving up something that you want to keep, especially to do something else or help someone

Inspired Values

Courage: Doing something that's difficult or dangerous, choosing to proceed in the face of obstacles or potential suffering or loss

Empathy: Feeling for the situation of others, sensing and sharing their emotions

Faith: Strong and lasting belief and trust in something or someone especially without direct observation or proof, a confidence that transcends a measurable contract

Generosity: Giving of your time, efforts, or resources without receiving back as in a trade, lessening of yourself for the benefit of others

Grace: An unearned gift of mercy or kindness, to be graceful is to give such

Gratitude: Realization and appreciation of one's good fortune, a thankful heart that returns kindness

Kindness: Consideration of others and caring for them

Patience: A steadfast peace in waiting without pressuring, an accepting of delay without anger

Thoughtfulness: Concern for the needs and feelings of others

Trustworthiness: Able to be relied on to do or provide what is needed or right

Wisdom: Using knowledge and experience to make good decisions and judgments

Life lessons are the actual experiences we've had that teach, reinforce, or establish our guiding principles and our core values. *Preferences* are things that we like, enjoy, or are comfortable with, but ultimately things that are neither transcendent nor right or wrong.

Capturing life lessons in written form can create a greater sense of unity and connection for a family and be a powerful way of capturing and passing the narrative wisdom of the family.

Elevation of Preferences to Principles

It's important to identify and understand the differences between guiding principles, core values, and personal preferences. In our desire to provide the best for our families, we can sometimes inadvertently elevate personal preferences to the same priority as core values or guiding principles and thereby damage the connection and relationships within the family.

For example, some families require in their estate planning that a child graduate from college to receive an inheritance. The guiding principle is self-reliance, the core value is hard work, and the preference is formal education. Education is a vehicle to achieve the guiding principle, but it certainly is not the only one. One child with a learning disability or one who is very entrepreneurial or hands-on could be strongly in line with the guiding principles of self-reliance and the core value of hard work, but her preference for the ideal venue is not formal education. Another child may thrive in school and spend a decade educating himself with no graduation in sight, ultimately to the detriment of those very same guiding principles and core values.

Another example is the issue of debt. Many clients are opposed to debt and yet many started their businesses with loans and used a mortgage to buy their house. Part of the discovery process in Entrusted Planning is to narrow down what you believe and why and how to pass on the most important lessons and wisdom without getting sidetracked

31

by personal preferences, especially because they can change over time.

Some parents go so far as to manipulate their children to act a certain way or to do a certain thing through their estate plan, such as choosing to leave assets only to those who work in the family business or only to married children. Attempts at behavioral manipulation through an estate plan are often very shortsighted. A more positive approach may be to use the same funds to encourage and foster the family's communal values, which may ultimately be far more of a gift to each member of the family than an attempt to force specific behavior.

We see the distinction noted in religious settings. *"In essentials unity, in non-essentials liberty, and in all things charity."* This quote, often erroneously credited to Saint Augustine, represents the philosophy of Rupertus Meldenius, a German theologian and educator, circa 1627. Identifying the guiding principles and core values of the family helps ensure that preferences are not elevated to principles, which could result in violating the spirit of the plan and devaluing the individuals in the family. An important part of the process of Entrusted Planning is the question, "What do we want our family to perpetuate and how can we allow for individuality in the advancement of our guiding principles?"

This is especially important in a multigenerational setting. There are differences among generations, especially with respect to preferences. Do you remember your parents telling you that your music was too loud or your clothes too weird? Preferences are generational, but guiding principles and core values are transcendent. They are aspirational and something the family can rally around. For example, a family might value forgiveness. If the family can put forgiveness at the center of their relationships, it can change the way they relate to each other for years to come. One of the obligations of a patriarch and/or matriarch of a family is to keep that family together. Often when the head of a family passes, the family has a tendency to lose contact if a solid foundation of generally shared guiding principles and core values have not been established.

Your core values and your guiding principles direct how you use your assets and they're worth spending the time to get right. You can sidestep this process by leaving your money to charity or engaging in traditional dump, divide, defer, and dissipate, but the lost opportunity to the family, especially to future generations, is tragic. You have a moment in time to decide to invest in your children, grandchildren, and future generations. You have the opportunity to create a dynasty by creating a family that's known for a series of successful members and the positive impact the family makes in the world.

Identifying Who You Are and What You Believe

The first step toward creating unity around who you are and what you believe is to identify your guiding principles and core values. Write them down, agree on them as a family, and be able to state them. Entrusted families see this, together with human capital, as a very important, if not the most important, asset of the family.

Rivets the Game™ is a simple yet powerful tool for helping a family or group identify their individual and shared core values. The results can also be used to help identify guiding principles and can be a powerful tool for launching into a motto, logo, mission statement, and the capture of life stories.

Remember that guiding principles are truths or beliefs that govern and dictate *why* we do what we do, and core values are ideals that we esteem, seek after, and cherish. They define *what* we do and what drives us to action.

As with each of the seven disciplines, this is a family exercise, best performed as a unit. Involving each member in identifying guiding principles and core values and in writing them down right at the outset gives the family a common language and framework. This is just as true whether your children are young or adults. The discussion can be adjusted based on age and maturity. The identification and agreement on guiding principles and core values are one girder in the bridge spanning the river separating generations. Consistent with Entrusted Planning, one generation does not dictate to the other. Rather, they come alongside each other to communicate and work together to determine the commonalities and direction of the family. Everyone's opinion is valued.

This doesn't have to be an antiseptic academic exercise. Use the common history of your family to engage. What connects your family? Where does your history lie? It may be a place—a family cabin or special vacation spot. Where does your family gather? Is it at horse stables, ski slopes, around the pool, or in the kitchen? Is there a special time of year, like Thanksgiving, or a special food you eat together? Use the commonality and history that already exists in your family to pull all the individuals together toward this important undertaking.

After you set out the simple prompt to identify guiding principles and core values, let the discussion wander. Don't control it. Let it drift into memories and family folklore. Pull the guiding principles and core values from the stories. Remember, you're creating unity and commonality, not dictating it. You want the participation and input of every member. We will lay out more specific strategies in subsequent disciplines, but in the meantime, think through what it might look like to begin this discussion in your own family.

A cohesive family identity can be hard to pin down. There may be a concept or notion of it, but there is something very powerful when a family sits down and collectively determines core values and guiding principles, especially as they begin to be implemented in the estate plan. This agreement not only helps the estate planning, but also generates a certain level of agreement, commonality, and understanding as they move forward. It also helps ensure that the family will remain cohesive should something happen and you're no longer around to hold the family together.

Vision Statement and Mission Statement

Although identifying and writing down your guiding principles and core values of the family are important, a list itself is not very motivational. Your list of guiding principles and core values should be used as a jumping off point to create a vision statement and a mission statement that will accomplish both.

A vision statement is aspirational—a statement of where you want to be. It is about the future: it focuses you on the direction you're going, your *North Star.* An example of a vision statement could be something like the following:

1. Go about doing good until there's too much good in the world.[2]

2. Love each other; help each other; believe in each other; wisely use our time, talents, and resources to bless others; worship together forever.[3]

Creating a vision statement isn't actually a new concept, although the term is a more recent concoction. Originally called *mottos,* they have been used by families and other groups for centuries to inspire, keep focused, and bind them together. Whether it's the Rothschild family's *Concordia, Integritas, Industria* (Harmony, Integrity, Industry) or the United States Marine Corp's *Semper Fidelis* (Always Faithful), a vision statement or a motto can help to bring purpose and direction.

---

2 Quote by Larry H. Miller
3 From the *Personal Leadership Application Workbook* for Stephen Covey's *The Seven Habits of Highly Effective People*

So what are good mottos? It could be as simple as Alfred Lord Tennyson's: "Love is the only gold." It could be lofty, like Polonius's: "This above all, to thine own self be true." Maybe it will be more practical, like Dory from *Finding Nemo*, who said, "Just keep swimming." Regardless, let your motto become your North Star—not just for your life, but also for your wealth and for your heirs.

A mission statement, on the other hand, sets out *how* you're going to achieve your vision. It's more practical; it's focused on what you do and how you do it. It's the map that leads you to accomplishing your vision. Here is one example of a mission statement:

- May our first word be adventure and our last word be love.
- We live lives of passion.
- We dream undreamable dreams.
- We are travelers not tourists.
- We help others to fly.
- We love to learn.
- We don't like dilemmas; we like solutions.
- We push through. We believe!
- We know it's okay to make mistakes.
- We bring people together.
- We are joy, rapture, yay![4]

---

4 From *The Secrets of Happy Families* by Bruce Feller

It's easiest to see and understand vision statements and mission statements in the context of their use in business. A vision statement doesn't change; it lasts throughout every iteration of the business. Business models and products, on the other hand, adapt to conform to the vision statement. Amazon's vision statement is to "be earth's most customer-centric company; to build a place where people can come to find and discover anything they might want to buy online."[5] Apple believes it's "on the face of the Earth to make great products, and that's not changing. We are constantly focusing on innovating. We believe in the simple not the complex."[6]

We see companies' vision statements reflected in how they do business. Amazon's policies are unflinchingly customer centric and their selection unparalleled. Apple's products are the stuff of legend.

Like a business, a family is a collection of diverse people with a common goal or objective. In fact, some families think of themselves collectively as a business and of each member of the family as an asset of the business. Although the level of volition may not be the same since we're born into our families, both represent a collective of diverse people with a common interest. If the collective can understand the core values and establish a vision

---

5 http://www.forbes.com/sites/patrickhull/2012/12/19/be-visionary-think-big/
6 Ibid

and mission, not only can that help to drive the estate plan, but it will also add to the ability to make a positive multigenerational impact.

Translating the guiding principles and core values identified by the family into a vision statement should be a group activity. Depending on how often your family is able to get together in person, you may need to draft the vision statement at the same time you work through identification of the guiding principles and core values. Both of these steps are important. Be sure to give your family time to digest and think through the principles and values, so they'll be able to express them before you move on to creating the vision statement. Ideally, the two exercises would be done at different times or at a multi-day family retreat to allow for a more rich discussion and a stronger result. A family coach or other professional trained in facilitating these discussions can be a powerful and effective tool in accomplishing these tasks.

A mission statement outlines how you're going to achieve your vision. Drafting the mission statement, which is more flexible and detailed than the vision statement, is part of putting dynamic governance into place.

Tree versus Hub and Spoke

We tend to think of families in a vertical fashion, like the family tree, starting with mom and dad then moving downward to kids and grandkids. In our experience, families are really more of a hub and spoke. Mom and dad are in the middle, the common connection point, with the kids radiating out like spokes. As the hub, mom and dad are in the center and keep everything together. Often, especially in families with larger amounts of net worth, the kids stay in line with each other and with the family while mom and dad have the assets. The wealth becomes the gravity that holds everything in place. As soon as mom and dad are gone, however, the connection point goes away and kids drift off in their own directions.

Guiding principles, core values, vision and mission statements remove specific people from the center hub spot and replace them with the family and their ideals. While mom and dad are living and controlling the financial wealth, the viewpoint is *we*; it's about the family. When mom and dad are pulled out of the hub and their wealth divided up, for each remaining family member, it suddenly becomes very much about *me*. Instead, with this approach, the next generation becomes the keeper of the hub, and their job is to continue to capture and pass on the vision of the family. Instead of one or two people holding the entire dynamic together, everybody has value. Everybody is together.

In a hub and spoke structure, only three things can keep the family together: the parents (who will one day pass away), the possessions (which may come and go and be diluted or divided), or purpose (which can transcend and bind for generations).

Capture the Family Story
and Collective Family Wisdom

"It's impossible to go through life unscathed.
Nor should you want to. By the hurts we accumulate,
we measure both our follies and our accomplishments."
—Christopher Paolini, *Inheritance*

Together with the more ethereal guiding principles and core values, it is also critical to capture the life lessons and history of the family that are the source of those principles and values. Tell the story of the family—including the mistakes. Often the bad experiences and failures are more powerful than the successes. Did you make financial mistakes and have to dig out of a deep hole of debt? What was your life like as you attempted to climb out of debt? What made that such an important lesson to learn? As you write your story or tell it to a professional biographer, use very specific details. Admitting your failures requires a level of transparency and humility, but courage can be found in the desire to allow others to learn from your mistakes and not repeat them.

This level of openness fosters communication and trust. It will impart the greatest wisdom to the next generations. We expect our children to make mistakes—there may be no better way to learn. However, it would be unfortunate if all of our children were to make the same mistakes. Encouraging an open dialogue within the family in which family members can educate each other on their respective failures would help prevent them from making the same mistakes.

Knowing Who You Are
Doesn't Mean Knowing It All

The fact that you're reading this book demonstrates that you're open to new ideas from those that work deeply in a particular area that you may not have had much exposure to in the past. Entrusted families are humble enough to know they don't have all the answers.

If we believe that we know everything, we shut off accepting or listening to new information—either from the outside world or inside our family. The most Entrusted families are those that are constantly asking, "What did you do? What do you think? What has your experience been?" They don't accept every input without question; they're discerning, but they're very willing to listen to the advice and counsel of others and figure out how that applies to their situation. It's a continuation of the humility required when you share your history. Entrusted families realize what they're good at and are willing to be coached in their weaker areas by someone with expertise.

At the end of the day, Entrusted families know who they are and what they believe, and they value and respect each individual. In some senses, this discipline can appear not to be related to the idea of estate planning at all, but it can form a powerful basis for Entrusted Planning—accomplishing the primary strategies of traditional estate planning to preserve and pass on wealth, but also so much more.

QUESTIONS TO CONSIDER

1. What are your core values?

2. What is your personal vision statement? Your family vision statement?

3. What is your personal mission statement? Your family mission statement?

4. What are a few of the most impactful lessons you learned in your life?

5. What would the process in your family look like to start building in this level of understanding?

6. What was the biggest mistake you have made in your life, and what did it teach you?

Core Values in Action: The Story of Alfred Nobel, A Case Study

Usually, great things in life are the result of hard work, deliberate action, and fierce determination. Other times, however, they're simply the result of a mistake. Alexander Graham Bell's breakthrough invention of the telephone happened, in part, because of spilled acid. A petri dish left mistakenly open led Alexander Fleming to the discovery of penicillin. When Wilson Greatbatch grabbed the wrong size resistor from a box of parts, instead of building a heart rhythm-recording device, he invented the pacemaker.

A mistake also led to the creation of the Nobel Prizes by Alfred Nobel. Nobel was born in Stockholm in 1833 to financially strapped parents. He was the fourth of eight children and was instructed, as were two of his brothers, in the field of chemical engineering. After several business failures in Sweden, Alfred's parents moved the family to Saint Petersburg. When Alfred was four and living in Russia, his father began manufacturing explosives, including a naval mine that could destroy enemy ships and submarines and defensively protect friendly vessels. The Nobels prospered and ramped up their children's education with formal schooling and tutors.

In the mid-1860s, Alfred invented an explosives detonator and a primary cap used to detonate secondary, more powerful explosives. Along with his younger brother Emil Oskar, he began experimenting with a highly volatile version of nitroglycerin. That early form of the chemical compound exploded at a family-owned factory in Sweden, killing Emil and five other people. After Emil's death, Alfred devoted himself to developing and manufacturing an explosive more stable than nitroglycerine. Through painstaking experimentation and research, Alfred was able to develop a solid, stable form of nitroglycerine, which he ultimately called *dynamite*.

Alfred's discovery of dynamite—and later gelignite, a gelatinous explosive even safer than dynamite—not only led to great scientific advancements, but also even greater wealth. Dynamite was used to connect cities and towns, mine natural resources to fuel development and growth, and to improve the lives and safety of those who worked in these dangerous professions. Dynamite was also used to create more effective and powerful bombs, landmines, and weaponry. It became a powerful force for good as well as for destruction.

Like dynamite, Alfred himself was something of a contradiction. He was a pacifist who owned, in addition to many chemical factories and businesses, nearly a hundred armament facilities. Although he had no children, he was thoughtful, deliberate, and wanted to make a meaningful impact in the world. He lacked any real formal education yet was proficient in six languages. When he wasn't creating even more powerful forms of explosives, he wrote poetry. His intent, however, was singular: To improve the lives of people and make the world a better, stronger, and safer place.

Alfred's two surviving brothers, Ludvig and Robert, were oilmen. They operated an oil company in Baku, Azerbaijan. By the late nineteenth century, they were producing 50 percent of the world's oil. The brothers—known as the *Russian Rockefellers*—invented oil tankers and modernized refineries and pipelines. By 1879, they were running Branobel, their oil company. They invited Alfred to join their partnership.

When his brother Ludvig died in 1888 at the age of fifty-seven, a French newspaper mistakenly reported that it was Alfred who had died. As a result, Alfred became one of the few people in human history to have the privilege, or curse, of reading his own obituary. Although he had invented dynamite in response to the tragedy of his younger brother Emil's passing, a French newspaper's headline perhaps summed up Alfred's life most succinctly: *"Le Marchand de la Mort Est Mort"* ("The Merchant of Death Is Dead"). The article detailed Nobel's life and declared that he had amassed his wealth "by finding ways to kill more people faster than ever before." The public response to his reported death led Alfred to a crisis of conscience. What would be the lasting legacy of this power he had brought into the world? How would he be remembered?

In an effort to reshape his financial and scientific legacy, Alfred directed that his estate be divided in two. A modest amount would go toward educating his nephews and nieces and rewarding several other family members, friends, and servants. The bulk of his "realizable estate," however, would fund the Nobel Prizes, yearly awards to be made to individuals or organizations notable for their achievements in physics, chemistry, medicine, literature, and the furtherance of peace.

Alfred Nobel had been devastated two times by the loss of brothers. He was determined to redeem the death of Emil by creating a safer form of nitroglycerin. He was also determined to redeem his own "death"—as well as the death of Ludvig—by restructuring his own estate planning.

Understandably, perhaps, Alfred's immediate family was not happy that he chose to leave the bulk of his assets to fund his prizes, and they even unsuccessfully attempted to challenge his will. Alfred, however, had carefully planned and was resolute in both his desire to establish a positive legacy and also in his concerns about the negative effects of inherited wealth, of which he said:

I regard large inherited wealth as a misfortune, which merely serves to dull men's faculties. A man who possesses great wealth should, therefore, allow only a small portion to descend to his relatives. Even if he has children, I consider it a mistake to hand over to them considerable sums of money beyond what is necessary for their education. To do so merely encourages laziness and impedes the healthy development of the individual's capacity to make an independent position for himself.

Chapter 3

Discipline 2:
Entrusted Families Prepare
the Family for the Wealth
and Not Simply the Financial
Wealth for the Family

*"Every affluent father wishes he knew how to give
his sons the hardships that made him rich."*

—Robert Frost

IMAGINE SLOWLY WAKING UP TO find yourself in
a warm sleeping bag on an otherwise chilly morning.
You slowly wipe the sleep from your eyes as you sit up
to absorb your environment. You realize that you're in a
small tent and that the wind is briskly blowing outside. You
find some warm clothes, quickly put them on, and then

cautiously poke your head out of the tent. To your utter shock and amazement, you look around to find yourself at the Mount Everest Base Camp in Nepal, a stark and bleak spot 17,500 feet above sea level at the foot of the world's tallest mountain. Before you can even explain your bewilderment to others at the camp, you find out that you're expected to immediately prepare to leave the base camp and trek across the shifting surface and cracks of the dangerous Khumbu Icefall in what would be merely the first part of your climb to the peak towering more than ten thousand feet above you.

People who have actually ventured to Everest to climb the world's tallest peak first spend countless hours preparing, training, practicing, and learning—well before they head to base camp. They've climbed other, smaller mountains and gathered and educated themselves on all the tools and skills necessary to successfully attempt an ascent. Although simply appearing at base camp without that preparation may sound ridiculous, too often children find themselves in that exact situation upon the death of highly successful parents. Instead of suddenly finding themselves at the Everest Base Camp, they find themselves sitting in the lawyer's office or standing in front of the employees of the family business. Unfortunately, they quickly find that they're unprepared, uncertain, and set up to fail.

Identifying guiding principles and core values and drafting a vision/motto and mission statement are the first major steps in the process of Entrusted Planning. The next discipline puts those principles and statements in motion. It keeps them from being as irrelevant as minutes from the last board meeting, which are usually put in a fancy folder and filed away.

Traditional estate planning focuses entirely on the money—it prepares the financial wealth for the family, which is treated as an amorphous blob and given no more humanity than names, birthdates, and numbers on a spreadsheet. Entrusted Planning, however, is not an event or a set of documents; it's a process based on relationship and connection. You define the expectations, you set the stage, and you prepare successive generations so that they don't find themselves shocked and unprepared for what happens next.

Entrusted Families Are Constantly Learning and Improving

"There are only two lasting bequests we can give our children, one is roots, the other wings."
—Stephen Covey

One of the characteristics of money is that it's a magnifier. It magnifies character, whether positive or problematic, and it's the job of older generations to shape and develop the character of younger ones. Too often, successful individuals don't take an active involvement in the formal or practical education of their children or mentees. They send their children to schools, public or private, and expect those institutions to teach them what they need to know—ignoring the vast storehouses of their own knowledge and the fact that their most important education most likely occurred outside of a classroom.

Often, very successful individuals don't like to talk about money. They're very private and opaque when it comes to finances, sometimes to the extreme of feeling embarrassed or ashamed by the wealth accumulated. Some presume their children will gain skills or abilities by osmosis or indirect exposure, but typically that does not happen. Instead of being secretive, you need to directly teach the lessons you've learned and help your children apply them in their own lives. There's great value in having your children understand how you're making your money, why you're making the decisions you're making, and what you've learned along the way. We've heard far too many times from overwhelmed clients, "Just let them sort it out when I'm dead." Sort it out they will—magnifying whatever bad habits their lack of preparation has taught them.

We know this can be a sensitive subject, because how we live may not seem consistent with what we tell our children and other family members. The reality is that children have the benefit of affluence because of their parents' hard work, effort, and risk-taking, but often the children don't make that connection strongly. They were often born into the elevated lifestyle. It can feel hypocritical to talk about sacrifice, self-reliance, and hard work when you've got a second home with a Porsche in the garage. Having your child save for a new toy or the cost of camp may seem difficult as you plan your trip to Hawaii.

There is so much more we can do to prepare our children for wealth and life than make them fly coach while you fly first class, and the best time to start is now. Entrusted families start preparing each member sooner rather than later, in age-appropriate ways. If your children are young, begin training them now, before they think they know everything. This preparation should include financial education and practical life-skills training. In fact, there are many excellent programs and training for affluent families for children as young as five years old through adulthood. Although capturing human capital and learning effective financial management can be done at any age, we are huge proponents of starting young and setting clear expectations in age-appropriate ways.

Although outside tools and resources can be extremely helpful, the key to preparing children is to remember that education is far more than just traditional school, and its most important elements cannot be delegated. Educating the children on how the older generation became affluent, what they did right, and what they did wrong, prepares the next generation for the transfer of wealth.

One way to accomplish this is to invite your children to traditionally closed-door meetings, even with the attorney, and start the kids early before a sense of entitlement kicks in. By starting early, children learn how your family views money and that it's really just a tool that can be used for good or bad. If you instill that type of philosophy early in children, it can influence the rest of their lives.

Of course, starting early works wonders, but no matter what your children's ages, a state of constant learning and improving will serve them in all areas of their lives. Immerse your children in meetings with advisors, even if they're told to sit there quietly and observe. You expose them to a bigger world as well as allow them to build their own familiarity with the advisors you rely on and may hope to continue to advise your family upon your death.

Education also includes addressing the unique issues facing the children of the very wealthy. By virtue of their public position, their spills, foibles, and problems will not stay in-house. They will hit the rumor mills, news, and Internet. Children of prominent families have the exact same problems as children from other, less affluent families—including drug abuse, alcohol abuse, and lack of purpose—but they're in the public eye and the crosshairs of the media. Entrusted families prepare their children for that level of scrutiny.

Entrusted Families Have Clear Expectations

As we mentioned earlier, hiding the ball regarding what children should and shouldn't expect can be insidious. A very small portion of children will presume they're inheriting very little and plan their life independently, finding their own path to financial independence. Left to speculation, most will assume they will receive a windfall—and that expectation exacerbates affluenza. Open communication, in age-appropriate ways, brings education, connection, and the passing of human capital to the forefront to address the transfer of wealth in all its forms. It does not use secrecy as a tool for avoidance.

Entrusted Families Value
Each Member's Individuality

*"We should not forget that it will be just
as important to our descendants to be prosperous in
their time as it is to us to be prosperous in our time."*

—Theodore Roosevelt

Accountability goes hand in glove with opportunity. When you give all your children equal opportunity to participate in the family via Entrusted Planning, they have to be held accountable to the entire process. It's not one discussion, one meeting, or one set of documents; it's a continuing relationship including transfer of wisdom and information. One element of Entrusted Planning is deciding what level of interaction is expected from each family member. If a particular family member does not want to be involved at that level, you must ask the question, how does it affect his or her participation in the benefits?

The responsibility inherent in accountability means that the possibility of failure and its consequences must be allowed. This can be a tough concept for families that have the ability to be a safety net for their children, young or old, in any circumstance. In one of the climatic scenes from the movie *The Dark Knight Rises*, Bruce Wayne is being held in a prison deep underground. His only chance of escape is to take a giant leap and grab on to a ledge across a wide span. Bruce ties a safety rope around himself and jumps. Falling short, he smashes against the wall. He trains and trains to build up his strength so he can leap further, but every time he jumps, he falls just short. Finally, he realizes the only way to clear the divide is to take the rope off. With the rope removed, he only has two options: make the jump or die. Only when he has no other choice but success is he able to make the jump and escape.

We see this frequently, and we suspect you do too. A child borrows money for a business or a house. Some children are fastidious about repayment, but some take the money as their due and just don't pay it back, despite promises to the contrary. Others try to repay but do so in a half-hearted manner. Parents make no real effort to collect and often feel sympathy for the tough financial position of their child. If the child behaved in this manner with a financial institution, there would be swift and heavy consequences, but the child knows that won't be the case with mom and dad.

The reality is that such children know that there are no consequences for failure to repay and instead use the money to fuel their lifestyle. No useful training and no skills are passed on this way. The training being given in fact is that mom and dad are there with the checkbook when a need or desire arises—no strings, no accountability, no responsibility and no consequences. When you don't face potential consequences, it's extremely difficult to succeed at something. Only when children are truly accountable and responsible will they value what they earn or receive.

Apathy, unfortunately, characterizes much of what goes on in estate planning. Motivation in general is one of the biggest hurdles to overcome in getting people to think about these issues. Entrusted Planning counteracts much of that apathy by dynamically involving all members of the family, but there can be a tendency to lose interest, especially if the interaction is framed as talking at length about death and taxes. Holding each other accountable includes holding ourselves accountable to continue to engage in the process, even as it becomes more difficult and the novelty wears off.

When you give your children and grandchildren equal opportunity to participate and contribute to the direction of the family, they need to be held accountable to continue on the path that has now been established. If they choose not to be part of the group, take notice and decide how that's going to affect what you do within the plan. Decide what engagement looks like and determine how to build in natural interactions over time that encourage the level of commitment and connection that brings this process to pass.

Entrusted Families Are More Concerned with Equal Opportunities than They Are with Equal Outcomes

*"There is nothing more unequal
than the equal treatment of unequals."*

—Unknown

Another way to prepare children is to avoid the desire to dictate or determine the path of *success* to children by attempting to engineer identical outcomes. Entrusted families create a sense of voluntary connection and allow individual identity. You must allow your children the freedom to make their own choices and to live with both the benefit and the burden of those choices. It is ultimately an issue of respect.

It's critical that children be allowed to select their own paths to success. Entrusted families set their children free to decide which path they're going to take in order to accomplish their goals and they help them along the way. They don't require children to carry on the family profession of being a lawyer, accountant, or doctor or to work in the family business. Parents should be mindful not to tie their identity with their children's successes or let their ego get involved in their accomplishments. In Entrusted families, it's okay if their daughter doesn't have a PhD. The focus in Entrusted Planning is on the equality of opportunity and not equality of outcome. Entrusted families realize it's okay if the outcomes are different, because each child had the same opportunity.

One child may love the outdoors and spend his time hunting and fishing. He might very well become a Yellowstone park ranger, and that's how he'll find fulfillment. Another may be business savvy and directed. She may become an extremely wealthy business mogul. Both lives have trade-offs. The second child is going to spend more time in the office under fluorescent lights, and the first is not going to have as much money in the bank as his sister. Entrusted families hold as a principle that each child can make a personal decision, accept the natural consequences of that decision, and understand that it represents an equality of opportunity.

This plays out in family businesses as well. The idea that all children should be treated fairly and equally should not extend to their position in the business. Skills and abilities should be evaluated and used to put the right person in the right position. To do otherwise is to attempt to exercise control and engineer an outcome rather than let the children choose where they individually find satisfaction.

There are no guarantees that even with careful thought, planning, and execution you can create a family united together in harmony. There are no guarantees that a child won't go off on a dangerous path. That said, if you fail to prepare the family for inheritance, the odds of disharmony and discord make negative events practically a certainty.

QUESTIONS TO CONSIDER

1. What did your parents do right when it came to preparing you financially for life? What could they have done better?

2. Do your children know what they should and shouldn't expect when it comes to your estate planning?

3. When it comes to allowing your children to fail, how does that make you feel? How willing are you to see that happen?

4. Do you include your family in decisions that affect the family's future?

5. If you have a family business, do you have a plan for how to balance the business with family? Do you have a plan for dealing with children who are inside and outside of the business?

Chapter 4

Discipline 3:
Entrusted Families Maximize the Positive Benefits of Holistic Wealth and Minimize the Negative Effects of Financial Wealth

ELEANOR: We can't all of us be as pretty as thou art. . . Come, here is a golden chain I will give thee if thou wilt lead me to thy mother.
GEOFFREY: No—no gold. Mother says gold spoils all. Love is the only gold.
—Alfred Lord Tennyson, *Becket*, Act 4, Scene 1

ONE OF THE HALLMARKS OF Western culture is the belief that "if some is good, then more is better." The answer to "Would you like one or two dollars?" is always two. The answer to "Would you like a 2,500-square-foot house or a 3,000-square-foot house?" is that the bigger, the better. For most of us, this makes perfect sense. When it comes to resources necessary for yourself and others, it's usually the case that the more resources you have, the better it is for everyone.

This belief is also foundational in the view of most people when it comes to inheritance and financial wealth transfer. In other words, if transferring some financial wealth to your heirs is good, then certainly transferring more is better. The reality is that most estate planning attorneys start with this premise as presumed and don't even discuss this fundamental assumption, which drives how the entire estate planning is designed, with their clients.

Correlated Relationships versus Inverted U Curve Relationships

The idea that if some is good, then more is better is what's referred to as a positive correlated relationship. For example, if you were to ask a football coach what his preferences are in terms of points that his team will score, he will always prefer more points to fewer points because more points gives him a greater chance of achieving his goal of winning the game. Exhibit 4.1 shows a simple positive correlated relationship in a graph form.

Other relationships work in a negative correlation (see Exhibit 4.2). Take eating cheesecake as an example. The first bite is typically the most enjoyable, and in fact usually

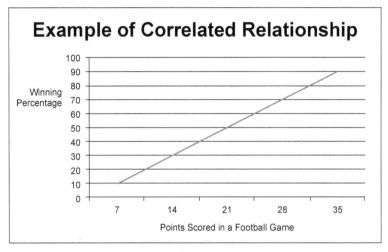

Exhibit 4.1

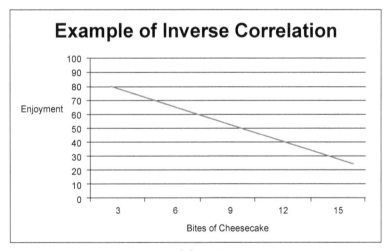

Exhibit 4.2

the first full piece is thoroughly enjoyed. That said, as you venture on to the second piece, you start to experience a decreasing return on pleasure. The fifty-seventh bite is not nearly as enjoyable as the first. Past a certain point, each bite of cheesecake is not as good as the one before. Economists call this the Law of Diminishing Marginal Utility, which basically says that as a person increases the consumption of a certain item, there is a decline in the enjoyment, or marginal utility, a person derives from consuming more of the item. A graph of the Law of Diminishing Marginal Utility would show a downward line.

Finally, some relationships are initially positive, but the relationship begins to diminish and eventually goes negative. If you were to chart this type of relationship, it would look like a hill that goes up, levels off, and then down, or what's referred to as an inverted U curve. Psychologists Robert Yerkes and John Dodson identified this type of relationship between stress and performance. When people are under little or no stress, they typically don't perform as well as when they're under an increased level of stress. That said, there is an optimal level of stress, and as you increase stress beyond that point, performance begins to be negatively affected. This relationship has been dubbed the Yerkes-Dodson Law and has been used by psychologists for more than one hundred years to identify a whole host of different relationships.

Take this actual example of an inverted U curve relationship in real life (see Exhibit 4.3)[1]. The X line represents cost and the Y line represents desired outcome, or at least what's presumed to be the desired outcome. As you can see,

---

1 Diagram is a simple approximation. See actual study for specific data.

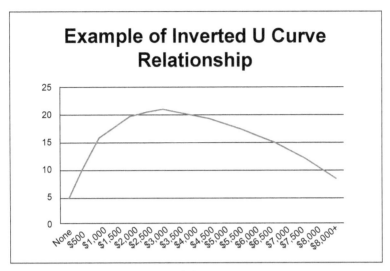

Exhibit 4.3

if you spend no money, you have less of a desired outcome than when you spend money. At about $2,000, however, something interesting happens. You begin to see reduced correlation and, as you spend more, a negative correlation begins. This is what is called an inverted U curve.

So what do these lines represent? The X line in Exhibit 4.4 is the amount spent on an engagement ring. The Y line is the length of the resulting marriage. For those who spent nothing for a ring, their marriages tended, on average, to not last as long as those who spent something. But, by the same token, as couples started spending more than $2,000 on wedding rings, the length of the resulting marriage started to go down.[2]

2 "A Diamond is Forever" and Other Fairy Tales: The Relationship Between Wedding Expenses and Marriage. Durstin (9/15/14), Andrew M. Francis and Hugo M. Mialon, Emery University.

Although this may be music to a prospective groom's ears as he debates how much to spend on a ring, the reality is that there are a multitude of other factors at play, and it's almost impossible to ever directly correlate only two factors.

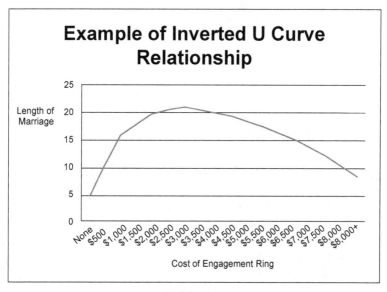

Exhibit 4.4

That said, as Malcolm Gladwell discusses in his book *David and Goliath*, when it comes to family income and its effect on current and future generations, just because some is good, more isn't necessarily better. Gladwell describes what he refers to as "desirable difficulties," those struggles and trials in life that act to strengthen, empower, and embolden. Although few of us would voluntarily choose struggles, problems, or afflictions, most of us would acknowledge that it's through those circumstances that we experience our greatest levels of personal growth. Having more wealth and more resources often means that you tend to face fewer of these extreme difficulties and trials. In fact, as parents, we often seek to help our children avoid or escape the trials and issues we faced in our own lives, and with more financial resources we're likely more able to assist.

Like most newly discovered wisdom, the concept of variable benefit as it relates to wealth transfer is not so new after all. In The Book of Proverbs—written nearly three thousand years before economists and psychologists came up with the terms *diminishing marginal utility* and *inverted U curve*—King Solomon said, "Give me neither riches nor poverty, but only my daily bread."[3] He saw that having too much can be as much of a curse as having too little. Much more recently, Warren Buffett said it this way: "A very rich person should leave his kids enough to do anything but not enough to do nothing."[4]

So what does wealth transfer look like as you advance along the wealth continuum? For argument's sake, assume that a given young-adult heir will most effectively and wisely use funds left to her. Access to ever increasing amounts of funds often follows a path that looks something like this:

1. Funds are first used to assist with education.
2. Next, funds are used to fully fund education, including advanced levels of education.
3. Funds are typically next used to assist with purchasing a house.

3 Proverbs 30:8
4 *Fortune Magazine* 25 June 2006

4. Funds may then be used to acquire or pay off a house or acquire a second residence.

5. Entrepreneurial heirs may use funds to start a business.

6. Eventually funds can be used to provide income for living expenses and general wants.

7. Finally, there are sufficient funds so that there is no need to work or produce income.

As you move along the financial continuum of what the beneficiary receives, you move from assisting in the launch of the beneficiary that can do anything to making it more likely she will fail to launch because she can choose to simply do nothing. The transfer of wealth goes from being a benefit to the point where it could actually detract from your family's principles and values. To use a sports analogy, with little or no financial resources, it can be difficult for an heir to even get into the game, while if they have too much, they don't ever need to play.

Although Gladwell discusses the potential benefit of these "desirable difficulties," he also acknowledges that not every person is equipped or able to overcome them. By the same token, transferring significant assets could keep an heir from needing to get into the game at all. The key is to figure out how to properly equip an heir without unintentionally sidelining her in the process.

Paradigm Shift

When we outline the inverted U curve as it applies to wealth transfer, we're invariably met with nods of the head from both individuals and families. Most of us instinctively acknowledge that, as the amount of wealth grows ever bigger, there can be diminishing and even negative effects. Once the inverted U curve is presented in terms of wealth transfer and the principle is acknowledged, the next question quickly follows: At what point does the line reach its highest marginal benefit and begin to turn downwards? Before you can identify how to maximize the benefit of inherited wealth, you first must ensure that you're able to meet your three primary financial responsibilities, which should be addressed in the following order of priority, or hierarchy:

1. Your first responsibility is to financially provide for you and your spouse (if any).
2. Your second responsibility is to raise and care for minor children.
3. Your third responsibility is to educate and successfully deploy young adult children.

This hierarchy of financial responsibility is static. In other words, it should be the same in your life as it is if you were to die. These priorities should govern how you view your wealth now and what you want to do to provide for your heirs. Many families may not be able to accomplish all three objectives, so it's important to focus on the first responsibility and then the second. It makes no financial sense to help a child start a business with a loan or co-sign on debt while a spouse needs to still be sufficiently provided for or to set up a trust to educate great-grandchildren while raising minor children on limited assets.

As you analyze your financial responsibilities, you can begin to identify what needs you can satisfy now, where you anticipate being in the future, and to what extent there may be excess assets and how to best deploy them. The hierarchy exists to ensure that wealth is not allocated to lower responsibilities while leaving needy family members with insufficient resources. The hierarchy can be especially helpful in blended families, families with a special-needs child, families who want to provide for extended family members and philanthropic interests, and families in which the spouses don't initially agree on how to allocate assets. A professional financial advisor can be critical in helping you with this analysis.

Once you've determined that you can successfully meet the first three responsibilities, excess assets can then be used to establish funds for opportunity-based planning (discussed more in Chapter 5) and/or philanthropy and social impact (discussed in Chapter 6). These decisions can and should be led by your vision statement/motto, your mission statement, your values, and your principles.

QUESTIONS TO CONSIDER

1. What are your thoughts on the potential effects of wealth transfer as the amount increases?

2. Do you believe that there is an optimal amount of wealth to be inherited by a person? If so, what is that amount?

3. What are your thoughts on the quotation from Warren Buffett: "A very rich person should leave his kids enough to do anything but not enough to do nothing"?

4. If you didn't deploy all your assets to your children or heirs at death, how would you want to see the excess assets used?

When Inheritance Goes Wrong:
Cornelius Vanderbilt, A Case Study

At the time of his death in 1877, Cornelius "Commodore" Vanderbilt was the wealthiest man in America. He started with one barge and went on to earn his wealth with railroad and shipping empires. He founded Vanderbilt University and left a sum of $200 million to his heirs, more than was held in the US Treasury at the time.

The Vanderbilt family followed the traditional estate planning model and passed on financial wealth. With that inherited wealth, Cornelius's son William expanded the railroad business and doubled the family fortune, but the other members of the family proved that there's no fortune so large that it can't be spent.

The next generations of Vanderbilts used their money to achieve prominence in New York's social scene and build some of America's most extravagant private residences in North Carolina, Rhode Island, and Manhattan. They held over-the-top fairy tale parties and raced yachts, sports cars, and horses. The Great Depression and newly introduced income and estate taxes took a toll, but other wealthy families like the Rothschilds, Rockefellers, and Du Ponts continued to prosper while the Vanderbilts floundered.

Within just thirty years of Cornelius's death, no member of the Vanderbilt family was among the richest in the United States; just forty-eight years after his death, one of his grandchildren is said to have died penniless.

In her memoir *Dead End Gene Pool,* Vanderbilt's great-great-great-great granddaughter Wendy Burden described The Burdens, a branch of the Vanderbilt family that inherited a portion of the wealth, as "a clan of over-funded, quirky and brainy, steadfastly chauvinistic and ultimately doomed bluebloods on the verge of financial and moral decline … rarely seen not holding a drink."[5]

CNN reporter Anderson Cooper is the great-great-great-grandson of Cornelius Vanderbilt, but he inherited nothing. His illustrious lineage didn't even give him a head start in his career. He began his career in journalism by forging a press pass and working for a small news agency.[6]

In 1973, the Vanderbilts held a family reunion at Vanderbilt University which 120 family members attended. There was not one millionaire in the group. A quote by William K. Vanderbilt, grandson of Cornelius, sums up the family's

5 http://www.countytimes.com/articles/2010/07/09/entertainment/doc4c35f45fe0795196685980.txt
6 http://www.earlytorise.com/how-the-worlds-richest-family-went-broke/

journey perfectly, "Inherited wealth is a real handicap to happiness. It is as certain a death to ambition as cocaine is to morality."

Chapter 5

Discipline 4:
Entrusted Families Focus on Flint
and Kindling, Not on the Fire

"A mighty flame followeth a tiny spark."
—Dante Alighieri

TWO ESSENTIAL BUILDING BLOCKS CAN be found
in virtually every personal success story: *flint* and *kindling*.

Elias and Ruth were hard-working parents of five children. Elias had worked in many fields, from construction at
the Chicago World's Fair to working a farm, running his own
business, and even delivering newspapers. Elias and Ruth's
fourth child, a son, was very artistic, and when he wasn't
working for his father for little or no pay, he was drawing and
doodling. He became so good that his drawings landed him
a job at age seven doing a portrait of a horse for a neighbor.

Recognizing his son's ability, Elias enrolled him in an art class at the Chicago Art Institute and later, after the family moved, in classes at the Kansas City Art Institute. His son was also a skilled performer, starring in the lead role in his school's production of *Peter Pan* and then dressing up as Abraham Lincoln and reciting the Gettysburg Address to every grade in his elementary school.

Aside from his artistic and dramatic abilities, the son was not much of a student and eventually dropped out after the ninth grade. A forged birth certificate by his mother allowed him to join the ambulance corps, and he eventually made his way to Europe to help with post-World War I operations for the Red Cross. While in Europe, he made extra money painting signs for canteens, souvenirs, and vehicles. Upon returning to the States, he continued to hone his artistic skills and eventually decided to start his own business. Skills and drive were not enough, however, and it took a loan from his older brother Roy to get his company launched. After a mix of success and failure, he eventually built a name, a brand, and a legacy unparalleled in American business. The son's name was Walt Disney.

Another family, headed by Arthur and Kate, lived on a beautiful homestead in Alabama, where Arthur was the editor of the local newspaper. Kate ran the home and cared for both Arthur's children from a prior marriage as well as the children they had together. When their first child, a daughter, was nineteen months old, she suffered a severe illness that left her unable to see or hear. They sought out the best experts they could find, including the famed Alexander Graham Bell, but all to no avail.

Finally, they found a determined teacher who was eventually able to communicate with the child and teach her not only to connect words with what she could feel, but also to read and communicate. Mark Twain introduced the young lady to Standard Oil magnate Henry Huttleston Rogers, who was so impressed by her that he paid for her education, enabling her to become the first deaf and blind person to ever graduate from college. The daughter's name was Helen Keller.

Paul and Clara were blue-collar workers living in San Francisco. Clara was unable to have children, so the couple looked to adopt, and eventually found Joanne, a young pregnant woman who'd come to San Francisco to give birth to a son. Initially determined to allow her child to be adopted only by college graduates, Joanne relented only when Paul and Clara agreed to set aside funds for the child's college education.

Paul taught his adopted son not just about mechanics but also the importance of attention to detail, aesthetics in design (both seen and unseen), and the value of knowing your product and what it's worth. When their hippie, vegetarian, unkempt son and some equally unusual friends wanted to start a business, they allowed their entire garage and several other rooms of their home to be turned into an assembly plant. The son's name was Steve Jobs, and in his parents' garage at 2066 Crist Drive, he started Apple Computers and changed the world.

Walt Disney, Helen Keller, and Steve Jobs are classic examples of excellence, perseverance, and determination. Each, however, took very different paths to success. Walt was born into tremendous poverty, Helen was born into relative financial security, and Steve grew up in a working-class family. Walt failed to finish high school, Helen was a college graduate, and Steve, despite all the money his parents faithfully set aside, dropped out of college. They all, however, had something in common: each had uncommon abilities that their parents fostered and developed through experience, skill development, and education; and each was given limited financial resources and assistance, which they took and multiplied many times over. The former, human capital, we call *flint*, and the latter, financial assistance, we call *kindling*.

A Fire or a Spark

Imagine you've ventured into the woods, found a spot to set up camp, and successfully built a roaring campfire. Fellow travellers stop and are warmed, protected, and comforted by the light and heat your campfire produces. Eventually, though, the time comes for these guests to continue on their own path deeper into the woods. To prepare them for their journey, you wouldn't hand them a flaming log. They'd have the log for only a short time and likely end up burned and lost. Instead, you'd give them the tools and resources to replicate your campfire so when they reach their own destination, they could make a fire for themselves.

Although a campfire may be a simplistic example, it's one that reflects the unfortunate reality of how too many people operate when it comes to transferring wealth. Transferring the fire itself—your financial resources—is transferring the *result* of your work and effort. However, the primary aim or objective is to keep the fire from burning out. When you give flint and kindling as opposed to the fire itself, you're instead transferring the means to the goal of success and self-reliance. The focus remains on how the fire started, how it was cared for, and how it grew. Flint and kindling transfers skills and tools so that successive generations can build their own roaring fire.

Traditional estate planning generally passes a lump sum of money, with minor or few conditions, which is basically transferring the ends. Entrusted Planning focuses on the means and allows the family members to create their own ends. It's based on the belief that the goal for successive generations should be self-sufficiency and independence, and so it focuses on the ability to replicate wealth and not simply on sustaining and consuming it. It's based on a simple but fundamental principle: successive generations, when given sufficient opportunity and means, can and will achieve on their own.

It's a positive and empowering perspective. It also allows for a much more meaningful conversation with the family, allowing them not just to see the success, but to also appreciate the effort it must have taken to create such a roaring fire. Focusing on the fire, however, is negative. It questions the ability or fortitude of successive generations and is based on fear and disbelief in those future generations.

Entrusted Families First Focus on Flint

Flint is a spark, or a starter. Education is certainly the quintessential form of flint, and it comes in many shapes and sizes and always begins at home. Traditional education is certainly of tremendous value and is obviously a prerequisite for many professions. Most people see traditional education as the first and best gateway to independence and self-reliance. That said, flint might also include nontraditional education such as work experience, internships, athletics, artistic development, and even travel. Education is and should always be seen as a beginning and not an end. No one would realistically say, "Because I have an education, I'm set for life. I don't need to do anything more." The value of education, of flint, is what it sparks—that is, the flame it starts.

For Walt Disney, flint came in the form of art classes and part-time drawing jobs that allowed him to hone his craft. For Helen Keller, it came in the form of a loving teacher who patiently and painstakingly taught a child who otherwise lived in darkness and silence. For Steve Jobs, the flint came not only in the traditional classroom but also at the side of his father and at the feet of neighbors who were electrical engineers and who were willing to share their time and their talents.

As discussed in Chapter 2, when providing flint to successive generations, it's important to make sure that preferences don't dictate the form of the flint. Highly educated parents tend to put increased value on traditional education. That's certainly a natural position to take. Traditional education was likely key to these parents' ability to achieve their level of success. Some children, however, are more suited to other forms of flint. Perhaps they're geared more toward experiential learning, volunteer service, an apprenticeship, or to the military.

The key in providing flint is to make sure it's understood, valued, and purposed. The most important education, though, (knowing who are who you are, what experiences have made you successful, your failures and the causes of these failures, and the overall philosophy of your family) is something only *you* can teach.

Even if you have the means to provide an unlimited amount of flint, consider placing limits on how much you actually provide. Some families have children pay a portion of their tuition and related costs, or limit their contributions to a certain period of time or a certain dollar amount. This allows each child to carefully consider and value his or her own educational experience. Even something as valuable as education can be degraded and even wasted. Think of it this way: just because you can do something for someone else doesn't mean you should, and just because something is valuable doesn't mean it will be valued.

Some of our other clients view a child's education as their job for the time they're going through that education. As such, these clients are willing to support the educational endeavors of their children and descendants, but only if these children are taking the education seriously and making reasonable progress toward a degree. This is also a fine way of viewing educational benefits bestowed on a child, but it does require vigilance and open communication about that child's progress and clearly articulated definitions as to what taking education seriously means and what constitutes reasonable progress.

Entrusted Families Provide Kindling

Kindling is a small amount of resource or material from which you can build a fire. Kindling captures the spark from the flint and gives it something to ignite. Kindling is a small starter, a little bit of savings that can be leveraged into something else, something greater. Kindling is never intended to do anything other than to precede something greater. It's a jumping-off point.

Kindling can take the form of funds for education, starting a business, a down payment for a first house, or charitable service. Again, it's different from traditional estate planning because it's just the starter, not the entire fire, and though it may be financial assistance, it has a specific purpose and intent.

For Walt Disney, his kindling was the loan from his brother Roy. Helen Keller received a scholarship from Henry Rogers so she could attend college. Steve Jobs's kindling came from a variety of sources: his parents provided a location for his start-up, and others provided loans and seed money to help his vision become a reality.

Providing kindling can be a tricky business, often much trickier than flint. As with flint, the key is that the kindling is a means to an end. The right balance of kindling is just enough to get things started, but not so much that it becomes the focus and ultimately a distraction. It's not uncommon to use a lot of kindling while building a fire that initially produces a great flame, but dies out without enough substance to keep it going.

The number of times you've provided kindling, the form it comes in, and what expectations come with that kindling are all decisions that must be carefully considered.

Flint and Kindling in Action

A client of ours recently demonstrated the power of providing flint and kindling rather than focusing on the fire. Years ago, he started an insurance brokerage company, which he slowly grew and developed. His son worked in the business from a young age and learned how to take care of clients and meet their insurance needs. After completing his formal education, the son came on board and worked alongside his father, continuing to build the business. When the time came for the father to retire, instead of simply handing over the business to his son, which the father could have afforded to do, he got a professional valuation and sold the business to his son at fair market value on an installment basis over time.

After a few years of timely payments, the son called his father, who was now retired and living across the country, and arranged for him to fly in so he could take him to dinner, just the two of them. Midway through that dinner, with tears in his eyes, the son proudly and gratefully handed the father a check for the remaining balance of the note. The son had a deep core value of integrity and, unbeknownst to his father, had been slowly saving money to pay the loan off early.

Our client later told us that this was one of the most meaningful moments in his entire life, seeing his son not just successfully running the business, but being so grateful for the opportunity provided him by his father that he sacrificed his own standard of living to pay it off sooner. It's a wonderful success story in the area of Entrusted Planning.

The son's education, both his formal schooling and the years of informal hands-on training he received working with his father, was the flint. The loan and opportunity to buy the business was the kindling. The result was well worth the effort—a thriving business and a practice that could continue into the future.

Some may ask, "Why didn't the father simply give his son the business? Why did he make him pay the same amount that he would have charged a stranger?" Although he certainly could have sold the business to his son at a discount or even gifted it to him, the father wanted to convey several important things. First, he wanted his son to make his own value proposition. He wanted to know that the son wanted and valued the business. Many second- and third-generation businesses fail not simply because those generations are ill-equipped, but because they're uninspired. They take over a business that doesn't interest them because they were handed the business or given it at a substantial discount. How many of us have bought something only because it was on sale and then have never worn or used the item? When the son paid full value, it showed his genuine interest in, and desire for, the business itself.

Second, the father, by expecting payment, was saying that he believed in his son and that he knew he could and would be able to fully repay the loan. He believed his son was every bit as capable as anyone to take over the business and fully pay what it was worth. The tears the son and father shed that night were as much about joy in all that the son had accomplished as they were about the pride the son felt because his father had truly believed in him.

Finally, selling the business to his son for its full value provided funds for the father to use as flint and kindling for his other children and for successive generations. Very often in family-owned businesses, one or more children will show a greater interest in taking over the business than other children, who may be more artistically inclined. Had this father simply given the business away, his other children would not have received a fair share of the estate from the father.

Some may argue that the other children were not entitled to an equal share of the father's estate since the son had been the one working in the business. This point is well taken but fails to address the additional time and attention the father spent with his son as opposed to his other children, educating him on the business itself (the flint), and the willingness to extend a loan to his son, who most likely would not have been able to qualify for a loan from a traditional lender (the kindling).

Family LLCs

Although the analogy of kindling in a family business context may be ideal, many children are not entrepreneurial, and starting a business may be the last thing on their minds. There are other ways to partner with children and provide opportunities to pass both flint and kindling.

Many of our clients, for example, establish a family-investment limited liability company (a family LLC). Typically, parent and child each contribute the same amount, which could be as little as one hundred dollars. The child is expected to earn his or her portion of the shared initial investment. The parent can, as necessary, loan additional funds at low or no interest so the family LLC has sufficient funds and resources.

The parent and child then collectively decide how to invest the funds—considering both traditional investments like stocks, bonds, or mutual funds and specialty investments like real estate or closely-held business interests. After repaying any loans and interest, additional earnings are equally divided between the parent and child. The objective is to allow the parent and child to work together to develop and plan and strategy for the funds and to jointly share in both the learning and the profits (or losses). The family LLC becomes a laboratory of sorts, where the generations can learn and experiment together.

This type of arrangement creates practical, educational, and mentorship opportunities with a finite amount of resources and risk. A family LLC structure can be used with young children, teenagers, and even adult children. The only differences may be the scale, complexity, and time frame of the investments. Whether the investments are ultimately successful or not from a financial perspective, the life lessons and mentoring opportunities are priceless. The term *family banking* is tossed around with ease these days by financial and insurance advisors. It can mean many different things and take almost limitless forms, but the family LLC can certainly be one of the implementation vehicles for a family bank.

Shotgun versus Mineshaft

The traditional model of estate planning is what we refer to as a shotgun approach. No matter the gauge of the shotgun, its force and power quickly dissipate the farther the shot travels away from the gun. That's the case with most wealth transfer. It can make a powerful and potentially destructive impact at the tip of the barrel, but its influence tends to quickly disperse.

An Entrusted Planning approach instead focuses on passing flint and kindling, accomplishing several important things at the same time. First, Entrusted Planning is a mineshaft approach. It keeps wealth concentrated and focused. It's designed to transfer opportunities to successive generations and trusts those generations to be self-sufficient and independent.

Second, because it stays concentrated, Entrusted Planning has a much greater opportunity to make a multigenerational impact. Assume, for example, that you have sufficient funds to allow one generation to supplement its income, take more extravagant vacations, and retire early. What if those funds were instead used to foster education, provide a small but meaningful down payment on a first home, or provide loans to start a business? How many generations could the funds last in that scenario? Two? Three? Four? What if those successive generations repaid and/or replenished these funds? Would it be possible for a family to create a perpetual opportunity machine? The answer is yes.

Finally, Entrusted Planning is built on a belief in successive generations. It says, "You don't need my financial wealth; you just need a start and an opportunity." That belief in a child, grandchild, or beyond, is powerful and can be life changing.

As we discussed in the previous chapter, when you're facing an inverted U curve situation, the key is to attempt to capture the high point and maximize the benefits and opportunities while minimizing the potential negative effects. Without any real opportunities for meaningful education or resources, it's very difficult to accomplish anything. On the other hand, by simply passing on the results of your efforts and not encouraging effort itself, you can create a host of negative consequences. The key lies in striking the right balance of flint and kindling to allow those you love to achieve and accomplish on their own.

Entrusted families see the passing of their assets as flint and kindling. They focus on opportunities, values, character traits, and behaviors that should be encouraged, not on assets or wealth. Flint and kindling says, "Let's start small. Let me teach you how to build and then let me give you the resources necessary to go and build on your own."

QUESTIONS TO CONSIDER

1. What kind of flint have you received during your lifetime?

2. What kind of kindling have you received during your lifetime?

3. In what ways could you foster self-sufficiency among your descendants?

Flint and Kindling: Mayer Rothschild A Case Study

Mayer Rothschild established his banking business in the 1760s in the back of a tiny apartment in an overcrowded alley in the Jewish ghetto of Frankfurt. He developed his financial house and spread his empire by installing each of his five sons in the five main European financial centers of Frankfurt, Vienna, London, Naples, and Paris.

Contrary to the custom of the day, Mayer did not *give* his sons money to begin their banking empires; he lent it to them. As additional interest, Mayer required his sons to inform him in intricate detail of their business and what was going on in their financial center. Mayer shared the information with all of his sons and, in so doing, created a network of current and consistent information.

A key to the Rothschild success was unity, a virtue Mayer instilled in his sons and that allowed them to run independent operations from great distances, acting as one firm that stretched across Europe. The Rothschild coat-of-arms includes a fist clutching five arrows, a reference to Mayer's five sons. Below the shield appears the family motto: *Concordia, Integritas, Industria (Unity, Integrity, Industry)*. The closeness of the Rothschild brothers can be seen in a letter written from one brother to another, which reads, "We are like the mechanism of a watch: each part is essential."

Each successive generation of Rothschilds continued the unity and sense of duty instilled by Mayer as well as his method of passing wealth. They focused on *opportunity* transfer and continued to loan—never give—money. They required repayment and production. The family met at least annually to share their successes and their failures in business, replicating the process Mayer Rothschild began in the 1700s.

The Rothschild fortune reached its height during the nineteenth century. It's believed by some to have possessed the largest private fortune in modern history. Today, Rothschild businesses span industries as diverse as finance, real estate, mining, energy, mixed farming, wine, and charities. In fact, the Rothschild name is synonymous with wealth and inspired the song "If I Were a Rich Man."

Chapter 6

Discipline 5:
Entrusted Families Are Generous

*"I've learned that you shouldn't go through life
with a catcher's mitt on both hands; you need
to be able to throw something back."*
—Maya Angelou

IN 2014, AMERICAN DRUG COMPANIES spent more
than $6 billion advertising prescription medications for
virtually any and every medical issue you can imagine.
Hardly a commercial break goes by without at least one ad
espousing the benefits of the newest pill. Imagine watching
a commercial with a couple walking hand in hand along
the beach. The voiceover describes a daily pill you could
take that lowers your blood pressure, increases self-esteem,
reduces the risk of depression, lowers stress levels, extends

your life expectancy, and dramatically increases your overall happiness, all with no side effects. Would you be interested in this medication, or would you simply dismiss the claims out of hand as fanciful and unrealistic?

This pill has actually existed for thousands of years. It's called generosity and its benefits are real and powerful.

According to a 2006 study published in the *International Journal of Psychophysiology*, people who gave social support to others had lower blood pressure than people who didn't. Even after a heart-related event, interaction with others helped recovery. The same study also found that people who gave their time to help others through community and charitable involvement had greater self-esteem, less depression, and lower stress levels than those who didn't.[1]

When you are generous, your quality of life is better and you live longer. According to a 1999 University of California, Berkeley, study people who were age fifty-five or older and who volunteered for two or more organizations were 44 percent less likely to die over a five-year period than those who didn't volunteer—even when taking into account other factors such as age, exercise, general health, and negative habits like smoking.

As you live a generous life, you are happier. In a 2006 study, researchers from the National Institutes of Health studied the functional MRIs of subjects who gave to various

---

1 (http://www.ncbi.nlm.nih.gov/pmc/articles/PMC2729718/)

charities. They found that giving stimulates the mesolimbic pathway, which is the reward center in the brain, releasing endorphins and creating what is known as the *helper's high*. Like other highs, this one is addictive. Biologically, generosity can create a warm glow, activating regions in the brain associated with pleasure, connection with others, and trust. As Saint Francis of Assisi said more than 800 years ago, "For it is in giving that we receive."

The People of Gander

The terror attacks on September 11, 2001, were one of the darkest moments in recent American history. Despite the tragedy, there were also many stories that day and in the days that followed of generosity, caring, and compassion. One such story took place in tiny Gander, Newfoundland, in Canada. In the chaos immediately following the attacks, American airspace was shut down and all planes in the air, whether commercial or military, were ordered to land as quickly as possible. Canadian airspace was also closed and ultimately thirty-eight commercial planes and four military aircraft were diverted to Gander, a town of roughly ten thousand people. Gander was the site of a large airstrip that was originally built during World War II as a halfway point for troops, supplies, and equipment between the United States and England.

The sudden and unexpected influx of aircraft on September 11 swelled the population of the town to nearly seventeen thousand. Unprepared for an extended stay and unable to access their luggage, passengers found a town that opened their homes, their hearts, and their pocketbooks. Residents provided housing, food, medication, and other necessities, all while refusing payment. They even arranged day trips and other outings for their new friends. So overwhelmed by the kindness and generosity of the townspeople, passengers in turn worked to establish a scholarship fund for children from Gander. Many lifelong friendships were created as fate brought together people who would otherwise never have even met.

Familial Benefits of Generosity

In addition to providing both emotional and physical benefits for the giver, generosity can also be a powerful tool for creating meaningful and lasting relationships, not just for the giver and the receiver, but also among givers as they engage in active service together. Generosity can also help bridge the generation gap. It can bring parents and grandparents together with children who may otherwise have very different goals, values, and beliefs.

Many of our Silent Generation (born between 1925 and 1945) and Baby Boomer clients (1946-1964) started and grew successful businesses. These businesses, though operated with the intent of making a profit, certainly provide significant social benefits in the form of economic development, infrastructure growth, employment opportunities, production, and tax revenue. Generation Xers

(1961-1981) and Millennials (1975-1995),[2] on other hand, often desire to have a more direct social impact and tend to be highly idealistic. These seemingly incongruent perspectives and objectives can often cause conflict, even in a family situation. By using the charitable tools we'll discuss in this chapter, particularly impact investing, generosity can be used to bring the generations together by creating commonality and connection and reconciling otherwise differing perspectives.

The Tools of Generosity

In addition to making direct charitable gifts and actively engaging in charitable service for others (either directly or as part of an organization), there are many tools that can be used to accomplish long-term charitable and philanthropic goals and objectives. That said, from a financial standpoint, they fall into two general categories: charitable-giving vehicles and impact investing.

Charitable-Giving Vehicles

The idea of a charitable organization that supports and encourages social benefits can actually be traced back to Benjamin Franklin, although the two earliest United States foundations (the Russell Sage Foundation and the Rockefeller Foundation) were not established until the early 1900s. If

---

2 Note that the names of the generations and years are often referred to differently and can overlap.

you are someone who has committed to charitable giving and have ever looked into establishing your own foundation to receive and manage your charitable assets, you've probably been overwhelmed with the complexity and options available for doing so.

Although most people may have heard about Section 501(c)(3) of the Internal Revenue Code, which allows individuals to establish charitable organizations and fund them with tax-deductible contributions, they may not realize that qualifying under 501(c)(3) is only half the battle.

Besides the ongoing maintenance of a 501(c)(3), which can be extensive, it also involves determining what type of charity you want to be, since there are several, each with its own advantages and disadvantages: private nonoperating foundations, private operating foundations, public charities, and donor-advised funds.

Private Nonoperating Foundations: A private nonoperating foundation, often referred to as a private family foundation, is the simplest type of charitable entity to set up. It can be established, managed, and directed by a select group of family members or individuals, and thus gives the donor and his family the greatest level of control. With that control, however, come numerous restrictions. Donors to private foundations are restricted from having any business dealings with the foundation, including the sale or leasing of assets to or from the foundation. Private foundations are also subject to a small tax on investment assets, a requirement that the foundation distribute a portion of its assets each year to other charities, and reduced deductions for certain types of contributions to the foundation. The largest private family foundation currently in the world is the Bill and Melinda Gates Foundation, with more than $40 billion of assets as of 2014.

Private Operating Foundations: Private operating foundations are foundations that directly engage in charitable activities, as opposed to nonoperating foundations, which primarily make grants and distributions to other charitable organizations. Charitable donations to private operating foundations are not subject to the same restrictions as nonoperating foundations, but operating foundations must meet certain technical tests regarding the use of their assets and their activities to qualify as such.

Public Charities: Public charities are charitable organizations that either engage in certain specific activities or receive contributions from a broad base of individuals or the public as a whole. Within the category of public charities, there are three main types:

1. *Favored charities:* These include schools, hospitals, churches and other organizations that have traditionally been deemed charitable in nature. These types of organizations are specifically outlined in the Internal Revenue Code and are subject to specific rules and requirements.

2. *Publicly supported charities:* These charities are those that receive at least one-third of their support from

the general public (that is, individuals other than directors and major donors). The American Red Cross, the United Way, and the American Cancer Society are examples of publicly supported organizations. Depending on the amount contributed, setting up these types of organizations can be difficult because of the challenge of getting a broad enough base of support to qualify.

3. *Support organizations:* Support organizations are charitable organizations that are organized and operated to support one or more other public charities. Support organizations can have a minority of its board of trustees selected by the donor, as long as a majority of the board is selected by charities that qualify as favored charities or publicly supported charities. Alternately, support organizations can have all of the members of its board of trustees selected by the donor, although to qualify it must meet numerous technical requirements and tests, which can often be difficult, and which require regular and substantial distributions.

Donor-Advised Funds: A donor-advised fund is a special type of public charity. Donor-advised funds are 501(c)(3) tax-exempt charitable organizations that allow donors to establish separate accounts to hold charitable contributions. The donor and/or the family retain the ability to advise on two matters: how the money is invested (subject to the options and choices that the fund provides) and the amount and timing of any distributions or grants from the account to other public charities.

Donor-advised funds can provide many of the benefits of a private family foundation, without the attendant administrative duties. Some donors do not want to engage in the more intense requirements of running their own private family foundation and for a usually small fee a donor-advised fund can remove that burden. Donor-advised funds can be general in nature or can be established to support certain affinity groups or geographic locations. Because of their ease of use, donor-advised funds are one of the fastest growing types of charitable organizations in the United States.

Impact Investing

Impact investing is the general term used for a business or enterprise that *attempts* to combine traditional for-profit investing with meaningful and positive social impact. It's a cross between a purely for-profit company and a purely social or charitable endeavor. From a family dynamic standpoint, it can be a great place for multigenerational interaction, mentoring, and development. It brings together the value of production and sustainability favored by many Baby Boomers with the value of positive and meaningful social impact favored by many Millennials.

Impact investing focuses on results. Typically operated as for-profit companies or low-profit limited liability companies (LLLCs),[3] entities engaged in impact investing are designed and operated to have a meaningful and positive social impact while also using revenue and some level of profit to fund operations and allow for scale. Rather than taking a portion of the proceeds of a successful business to use for charitable purposes, the business itself provides a direct benefit. Historically, individuals and families would separate their for-profit business activities from what they did from a charitable standpoint. Andrew Carnegie built vast wealth as a *robber baron,* but he also gave away money to build libraries and schools and to support other public institutions. Impact investing blurs the lines between earning wealth and using wealth to benefit others. It asks, "Why does one have to be to the exclusion of the other?" It integrates the whole person and even the family into their business and life activities.

The Paradigm Project, founded by Greg Spencer and Neil Bellefeuille, is a wonderful example of the blend between a sustainable business model and meaningful social impact. In 1996, Spencer co-founded Blue Source with his partner, global entrepreneur Bill Townsend. The company was formed to help create and establish a carbon-offset market, with the goal of reducing overall carbon emissions and has been

---

3 An LLLC is a hybrid type of entity that many states have adopted to address the concern that most LLC laws are designed with the notion that the entity should be operated only and motivated solely for profit. An LLLC is allowed to operate and make decisions with social and charitable considerations in addition to purely profit motivations.

a leader in developing offset projects in forestry, methane abatement, transportation, coal mine methane capture, and carbon capture and sequestration (CCS).

Although Blue Source creates significant environmental benefits, the business is not designed to achieve other social benefits, particularly a direct connection to the needs of the rural poor, who are likely to be most affected by climatic changes due to their inability to switch vocations or find alternate sources of income.

In evaluating this limitation, Spencer sought a commercial approach to using carbon finance to help achieve social and economic development in emerging economies. In the process, Spencer discovered an emerging industry in rural Africa involving household cooking. Roughly three billion people in this world—literally half the population of the planet—still boil water and cook their meals over an open fire, and many do that indoors. As a result, women and children die from the cumulative effects of smoke inhalation and families spend vast amounts of time, money, and energy to gather and purchase fuel. Forests are also rapidly disappearing all over the world as wood is harvested and collected at unsustainable rates. As a result of all of this burning, massive quantities of greenhouse gas emissions are also released into the atmosphere every year. The Nature Conservancy estimates that the rural poor generate an estimated 25 percent of global carbon dioxide emissions. That's more than every car, bus, train, and plane on the planet emit combined.

In addition, according to the World Health Organization, more than four million women and children die every year from lower respiratory disease related to indoor cooking smoke. In fact, pneumonia from lower respiratory disease is the number one killer of children under five years old globally—not AIDS or waterborne illnesses or malnutrition, but pneumonia from exposure to indoor cooking smoke. In many areas of the world, women walk more than ten miles per trip and spend more than thirty hours per week collecting wood, carrying forty- to sixty-pound bundles back to their homes. Families who purchase fuel often spend 30 percent or more of their annual income on cooking fuel alone.

Making it easier to cook and boil drinking water would improve household income by reducing fuel purchases and improve productivity by freeing up the time formerly used to gather wood. It would also reduce deforestation and carbon emissions and provide a health benefit by reducing exposure to ash and other byproducts of open flames.

At the confluence of carbon-emission reduction, meaningful social impact, and sustainability, Spencer helped to form the Paradigm Project, which designs, manufactures, and sells high-efficiency cookstoves in Africa. Replacing open fires with fuel-efficient stoves dramatically impacts lives and reduces degradation of the environment. A simple, efficient stove can reduce wood or charcoal use by 40 to 50 percent and toxic emissions by up to 70 percent. As a result, lives, time, and money are saved, deforestation is slowed, and greenhouse gas emissions are significantly reduced.

In addition to the social and environmental benefits at the household level, the Paradigm Project creates jobs, sustainability, and replication by selling an affordable but nevertheless profitable product. Earnings from the sale of stoves are used to continue the cycle of positive impact in other communities. In addition, the Paradigm Project captures the value of the carbon-emission reduction in the form of carbon credits and then monetizes those credits to reduce product cost to the consumer and increase returns to the investors. The Spencers also value the fact that their son has taken an active role in the Paradigm Project. Their son Greg shares in many of the passions of his father, and he is mentored by Greg Sr., and others on the management team. As the Paradigm Project continues to grow, the teams, along with family members, all take an active role in helping move the goal and vision along.

The Paradigm Project is a great example of impact investing, but it's not the only one. More and more enterprises are improving multiple bottom lines by creating a culture and business model to simultaneously achieve financial and social returns. This type of structure can be found in the fields of education, social welfare, the environment, and medicine.

Like any investment or charitable gift, it's important to carefully analyze and evaluate the business model and structure of an impact investment. Questions to consider when evaluating an impact investment include:

1. What is the anticipated social impact and benefit? Can these benefits be accurately measured? How do the benefits align with my goals, values, and beliefs?

2. What is the revenue model for the enterprise? Is it sustainable? Scalable? Can competitors easily replicate it?
3. What is the form of the investment? Is it a loan or a capital/equity investment?
4. What are the skills and qualifications of the leaders and directors of the enterprise? Do they have the necessary skill sets and passions?
5. Does this enterprise capture my interests and passions? Can it be used to help foster meaningful connection and mentoring within my family?

Although impact investing can provide a wide range of investments, employing that label should not be an excuse to have an incomplete business plan or model. Even with a sound and positive social component, a potential impact investment will likely be sustainable only if it is operated using best business practices, and is able to stand up to the scrutiny that other types of investments do.

Creating a Culture of Generosity

The personal and social benefits of generosity can be further enhanced when you also engage family, coworkers, and others by creating a culture of generosity though collaboration. Examples of this include grant-making certificates, matching donations, impact investing LLCs, and philanthropy therapy.

Grant-making certificates: One family we work with developed a plan to start engaging everyone in the family in giving. For each birthday, the parents give the children and grandchildren a small gift and a *grant certificate*, which gives the recipient the ability to designate the charitable organization that will receive the grant amount. The only requirement is that the child or grandchild think about and research the organization and inform the parents of their selection and reasons. It has become a great way to partner with family members and talk about generosity.

One of the grandchildren, a second grader, recently selected the Leukemia and Lymphoma Society. The family was quite surprised by the selection, unaware that the child even knew that such diseases existed. The grandchild explained that one of his classmates was recently diagnosed with leukemia and was undergoing treatment, and he wanted to help his classmate. The act of giving the gift created not only a sense of other-centeredness in the grandchild but also connection and communication between the child and his grandparents.

Matching donations: Several families we work with have also established a charitable donation-matching program, in which the parents will match charitable contributions by their children up to a certain amount. This helps to engage the children by having them earn funds and donate those funds, while also working to leverage and magnify the ultimate gift. Depending on the age and amounts, the donations could even be leveraged. A young child could save up fifty dollars from working around the house or doing yard work, and the parents could match it with $500 of their own funds. Regardless of how the arrangement is structured, giving of your own time, talents, and resources is also more engaging and impactful than simply giving other people's money away.

Impact investing LLC: In the previous chapter, we discussed the use of family LLCs to allow family members to engage in entrepreneurial activities together. This can also be done in the context of impact investing, wherein parents establish and fund a family LLC and, together with one or more children, the funds are invested in impact investments. A family LLC focused on impact investing can be a powerful incubator for mentorship, community, and philanthropy, and though funding the LLC will likely not achieve a tax deduction, operations and investment decisions are not burdened by the numerous restrictions of a foundation or even the lesser restrictions of a donor-advised fund.

Philanthropy therapy: Philanthropy can also be used to help families going through difficult situations. One family we worked with had amassed a very large estate due to a preceding generation's sale of a highly lucrative business. The next generation had been instilled with many of the family qualities that made the previous generation wealthy. However, as the third generation was being raised, less emphasis was placed on the value of hard work and focus on the family's legacy was lacking. Being raised in the lap of luxury, with no real direction being provided to that generation, a few of the grandchildren started down unproductive paths. Issues of substance abuse, school dropouts, and problems with law enforcement were unfortunately commonplace.

The second generation wanted to do something about this situation, so we worked to assist them in developing a plan to address the apathy that had become rampant in the family. This family had been generous with charitable giving in the past, so we knew there was interest in philanthropy. We suggested they leverage this philanthropy so as to motivate the next generation. Instead of the normal amount of charitable donations the family would give directly to organizations each year, we established a system wherein each grandchild was given the right to direct an equal portion of that charitable amount to a qualified charitable organization of their choosing.

However, the next generation was not simply given a blank check: requirements had to be met before the donation would be made. The grandchildren would have to meet with the charitable organization and research the organization's charitable purposes. If the charity had a physical location, like a homeless shelter, the children would have to visit the location. This not only nudged the children out of their comfort zones, but it also expanded their network of people and exposed them to both those who were far less fortunate and those who were doing good in the world.

The grandchildren would then need to prepare and deliver a report to all members of the family who wished to participate, thereby empowering them to educate others, rather than just sitting back and directing. This approach fostered togetherness within the family, and it's still working today.

Although we would love to be able to tell you that this work has resulted in *all* family members getting on the straight and narrow, it hasn't. But four of the previously at-risk grandchildren have now started their own charitable endeavors and have become large members of the charitable community, implementing similar goals within their own family planning, now into the fourth generation.

Conclusion

Generosity is a tool that can be used to provide innumerable benefits to the giver, recipient, and even to others involved in the process. It can be a powerful force to bring families together, create a sense of purpose, foster greater community, and create results that have scope and duration far greater than those from a purely financial investment. It can also be a tool to bring generations together and foster meaningful and impactful relationships.

QUESTIONS TO CONSIDER

1. What does generosity mean to you?

2. What impact has generosity had in your life, either as a giver or a recipient?

3. In what ways could generosity positively affect your family?

4. Have you seen examples in your life when activities have had both financial and social benefits?

5. What charitable or social causes could you see being supported by your family?

A Legacy of Generosity:
Saint Wenceslas, A Case Study

"Good King Wenceslas looked out on the feast
of Stephen, when the snow lay round about deep and
crisp and even; brightly shone the moon that night though
the frost was cruel, when a poor man
came in sight, gath'ring winter fuel."
—John Mason Neale

In the tenth century, the Duke of Bohemia, in what is now the Czech Republic, sat down to his dinner during a cold winter's night. As the story goes, he looked out into a blizzard and saw a man who was clearly quite poor gathering fuel for a fire. Shocked that anyone would be out on such a cold night, he called to his page and asked about the man. Discovering that man lived quite far away, the duke quickly gathered wood, food, and wine and set off to help the man, with the page following.

Through the snow and the fierce winds, the duke pushed ahead. His page struggled to keep up. The duke instructed him to follow his every footstep in the snow so the page could continue on in the fierce storm.

The duke did not limit his generosity to one single night. He was known throughout his short twenty-eight years for his generosity to widows, orphans, and prisoners, and although he was never a king while he lived, the duke was posthumously bestowed the title of king and declared a martyr and saint. Stories of his life had a powerful influence on the High Middle Ages and helped to establish the concept of *rex justus,* or righteous king—that is, a monarch whose power stems mainly from his great piety, not merely from his princely vigor.

Today, we know the duke as Saint Wenceslas, honored in the popular Christmas carol ("Good King Wenceslas"). Although in power for just ten years more than a thousand years ago, his name is synonymous with generosity and humility. He is the patron saint of the Czech Republic and his legacy lives on through the tradition of charitable giving on Boxing Day, the day after Christmas.

> *Good King Wenceslas looked out*
> *On the feast of Stephen,*
> *When the snow lay round about*
> *Deep and crisp and even;*
>
> *Brightly shone the moon that night*
> *Though the frost was cruel,*

When a poor man came in sight,
Gath'ring winter fuel.

'Hither, page, and stand by me,
If thou know'st it, telling
Yonder peasant, who is he?
Where and what his dwelling?'

'Sire, he lives a good league hence,
Underneath the mountain,
Right against the forest fence,
By Saint Agnes' fountain.'

'Bring me flesh and bring me wine,
Bring me pine logs hither,
Thou and I will see him dine
When we bear them thither.'

Page and monarch forth they went,
Forth they went together,
Through the rude wind's wild lament
And the bitter weather.

'Sire, the night is darker now
And the wind blows stronger;
Fails my heart, I know not how,
I can go no longer.'

'Mark my footsteps, good my page,
Tread thou in them boldly:
Thou shalt find the winter's rage
Freeze thy blood less coldly.'

In his master's steps he trod,
Where the snow lay dinted;
Heat was in the very sod
Which the Saint had printed.

Therefore, Christian men, be sure
Wealth or rank possessing,
Ye who now will bless the poor
Shall yourselves find blessing.

Chapter 7

Discipline 6:
Entrusted Families Preserve
and Protect Wealth

"To (Pre)serve and Protect"
—Slightly modified motto of the
Los Angeles Police Department

THE COMBINED EROSIVE POWER OF water, wind, and gravity has brought down once mighty mountains, shaped entire continents, and caused even massive islands to eventually succumb to the sea. Recent erosion surveys of Niagara Falls, which began in 1842, report that the annual average rate of erosion of the Horseshoe Falls has dropped from 3.8 feet per year to less than one foot thanks to increased water diversion and anti-erosion steps. The projected rate of erosion for the future is even lower, down to one foot every *ten* years. Without taking those thoughtful remedial steps, however, Niagara Falls would have devolved into a shadow of its former self, and its current awe and splendor eventually would have been completely lost.

Preserving and protecting financial wealth requires an understanding of, and a solid plan for, counteracting the three primary forces that erode wealth over multiple generations. Just as water, wind, and gravity work to erode natural monuments, three forces work to erode financial wealth over multiple generations:

1. The division of assets among the generations
2. Transfer taxes and capital gains taxes
3. Business risks and third-party attacks

Studies have shown that as a result of these three forces, financial wealth doesn't last past the third generation in 90 percent of high-net-worth families.[1] This truism has sometimes been expressed as "Shirtsleeves to shirtsleeves in three generations," an American translation of the Lancashire proverb, "There's nobbut three generations atween a clog and clog." Each of these threats to the retention of financial wealth must be addressed and counteracted.

The Division of Assets Among the Generations

Historically, wealth was maintained and concentrated for the collective benefit of the family as a whole typically, in the

---

1 (http://www.wsj.com/articles/SB10001424127887324662404578334
663271139552, http://www.corpmagazine.com/special-interests/family-
business/shirt-sleeves-to-shirt-sleeves-in-three-generations/)

western world, in the form of land and titles. As financial wealth became removed from the means in which it was produced (that is, became commoditized), wealth became much easier to divide and dissipate at each generational level. Instead of owning a part of the family farm or business, now the next generation could simply sell illiquid assets (if any) and divide the liquid and marketable assets among the next generation.

The diminishing effect is best illustrated by an example: two parents have four children, who each have four children, who then each have four children. Without taking into account any other factors—including tax implications—when the assets are divided, each child on the first generational level would receive one-quarter of the original estate from their parents. Grandchildren would receive one-sixteenth each and great-grandchildren, one-sixty-fourth. Presuming a $10 million estate in which the principal is preserved and only the income spent, each great-grandchild would receive slightly more than $150,000.

The effect is like a shotgun. Far enough away from a shotgun blast, you won't even feel it.

Taxes

In America, any discussion of taxes needs to be very specific because we pay many direct as well as disguised taxes. One article recently identified ninety-seven different types of fees and taxes that Americans pay.[2] When it comes

---

2 (http://www.zerohedge.com/news/2014-03-25/list-97-taxes-americans-pay-every-year).

to estate planning, there are five types of taxes that cause the most erosive effect on multigenerational financial wealth transfer:

1. *Federal estate tax:* The federal estate tax is a tax on assets over a certain amount owned by an individual at death. The amount of the tax and the exemption that can be used against the tax has been in a constant state of flux since the latest iteration of the federal estate tax was introduced in 1916.

2. *Federal gift tax:* Introduced in 1932 as a means of restricting the transfer of funds that would otherwise be subject to the federal estate tax, the federal gift tax is a tax on the gratuitous transfer of funds from one person to another during life. The tax rate mirrors the federal estate tax rate, and in addition to an annual exclusion from the tax, an individual can use part of the estate tax exclusion amount against lifetime gifts.

3. *Federal generation-skipping transfer tax:* This tax, introduced in 1976, is a tax imposed on the transfer of assets, either at death or during life, to an individual who is more than one generation removed from the donor. This tax is in addition to the applicable estate or gift tax. The compounding of the estate tax and generation-skipping transfer tax can be as high as 90 percent of the amount of the assets transferred. It is intended to ensure that tax is imposed on the transfer of assets to each generation and that the applicable estate or gift tax is not skipped.

4. *State estate or inheritance taxes:* In addition to the federal estate tax, several states have an additional estate or inheritance tax. An inheritance tax is a tax on the recipient of a transfer of assets on death, as opposed to an estate tax, which is a tax on the estate (or effectively on the donor).

5. *Capital gains tax:* This is a tax on the difference between the purchase price of an asset (the basis) and the sales price. In general, when an individual dies the assets that are subject to estate tax receive a step-up in basis to avoid the otherwise potential double taxation of an appreciated asset that is sold after death. Some assets, most notably retirement plan assets, do not receive a step-up in basis at death.

To illustrate how just one of the taxes listed here, the federal estate tax, can wear away wealth, let's look at our hypothetical family again. This time, let's grow the size of its estate to $100 million, again with the principal preserved and only the income spent. While the first generation would pay a 40 percent estate tax (the current estate tax rate), the second generation would pay an effective 64 percent estate tax (40 percent on 60 percent remaining assets) and the third generation would pay a 78 percent estate tax. Coupling the erosion due to division, (outlined above), with the estate tax effect, a $100 million estate in which the principal is not consumed is nevertheless reduced to $343,750 for each great-grandchild—presuming none of their parents or grandparents gets sued or divorced. That's .34% of the original amount of wealth at the great-grandparents' level.

Business Risks and Third-Party Attacks

Divorces, outside creditors, medical issues, and other outside factors can also have a tremendous effect on the multigenerational transfer of wealth. This is a wild card that, left unchecked, can literally wipe out financial wealth at any generational stage of the transfer. The more assets you have, the more likely you are to be involved in litigation. Personal guarantees can bring with them a tremendous level of potential risk as well, especially considering that most co-signed debt is done on a joint-and-several liability basis, meaning that a creditor can go after the person with the most assets and leave it to him to seek recourse against his fellow borrowers.

A Word About Asset Protection

The term *asset protection* often means different things to different people. To some people, asset protection means trying to hide assets or avoiding legitimate debts and obligations. To others, asset protection means attempting to set aside or protect certain assets from the risks associated with other unrelated business activities or ventures.

The most effective asset protection simply involves a variety of planning techniques designed to place certain assets outside of the reach of potential future, unknown creditors. This is most often accomplished by the compartmentalization of risk and the strategic ownership of assets. The best asset protection strategy can be fully disclosed and yet still fully effective. Asset protection is not an attempt to hide assets or to misrepresent the truth of the particular situation. Property and Casualty Insurance is always the first and most important asset protection tool, but some situations aren't covered by insurance or the situation involves risk beyond the coverage limits of the particular policy.

The two primary factors to consider when doing asset protection planning are the following:

1. *The type and nature of assets:* Many assets provide natural asset protection. For example, qualified plan assets such as 401(k)s, 403(b)s, IRAs, and Roth IRAs have protections under federal law and most state laws. In addition, life insurance policies are also afforded a certain amount of state law protection. Other assets, however, can be more difficult to protect, and state law has a tremendous effect on the level of protection afforded to those other assets.

2. *The types and sources of risks:* Risks typically come in two forms. The first is asset-based: risk that someone incurs as a result of the assets owned. Through the use of corporations and limited liability companies, you can compartmentalize those assets with high risk from other assets. The second is direct: risk that someone incurs from personal and professional activities. There are multiple strategies to deal with this type of direct risk from the fairly straightforward to the most advanced and sophisticated plans.

Tools to Preserve and Protect Financial Wealth

Although the corrosive effect of division, taxes, and third-party attacks is real and powerful, there are tools that can be used to protect assets and preserve the financial assets of a person's estate so that those funds can be used to pass on flint and kindling (Chapter 5) and encourage and support generosity (Chapter 6). Although your estate planning should be guided by your goals, values, and beliefs, you need an actual legal structure to hold assets, manage investments, and make distributions pursuant to your stated objectives. When effectively implemented and operated, the two primary tools—trusts and business entities—are powerful asset protection tools that have been used by families and businesses for hundreds of years. Although the purposes and principles outlined in the prior chapters create the heart and soul of your estate planning, it is these tools that create the skeletal system that can hold and sustain your financial resources.

Trusts

Trusts have been used for hundreds of years to effectively hold, manage, and protect assets. Trusts are the only type of mechanism that can engage in business and own property without any type of public filing. Trusts are established by one or more individuals, called *settlors*, who determine the terms and conditions in which the *trustees* hold and manage assets for the benefit of the *beneficiaries* of the trust. Trusts divide the assets they hold into three separate components:

1. *Control:* The control of assets owned by a trust is given to the trustee(s) of the trust (described in more detail below). They are responsible for the investment, management, and distributions of the assets of the trust to the beneficiaries, pursuant to the terms of the trust.

2. *Use:* The beneficiaries have the ability to receive and/or use the assets of the trust as determined by the trustees. A trust can own real property, business interests, marketable securities, and even vehicles and allow the beneficiaries of the trust the right to use and enjoy those assets.

3. *Ownership:* Although the trustees manage and control the assets and the beneficiaries have the ability to use and enjoy the assets, the trust itself is the legal owner of the assets. This means that properly structured trusts can hold and manage assets for the benefit of beneficiaries without the assets of the trust being subject to the claims of potential creditors of either the beneficiaries or the trustees.

Domestic Asset Protection Trusts

Domestic asset protection trusts (DAPTs) are trusts established in certain jurisdictions to provide unique benefits not previously found in trusts established in the United

States. In the late 1990s, South Dakota and Alaska became the first states to pass new trust laws to compete with offshore trusts that were being used by thousands of US citizens for estate planning and asset protection. Since then, several other states have passed similar laws. These laws regulating DAPTs allow individuals to do the following:

1. *Continuance in perpetuity:* DAPTs are sometimes referred to as "dynasty trusts" because DAPT laws allow trusts to continue for multiple generations. Previously, state trust laws limited the term of a trust to no more than twenty-one years after the death of the last surviving initial beneficiary of the trust (the so-called Rule Against Perpetuities).

2. *Asset protection from future creditors:* In most states, if you establish a trust for the benefit of yourself (a so-called self-settled trust), then the assets of the self-settled trust are subject to the claims of your creditors and included in your estate for estate tax purposes. States with DAPT statutes have changed their laws to allow individuals to establish trusts and have those assets protected from the claims of future unknown creditors, provided the transfer of assets to the trust is not a fraudulent conveyance—any transfer that is has the purpose or effect of hindering, defrauding, or delaying the legal collections efforts of a creditor. Each state has different requirements for such protection to apply.

    If properly formed and operated, then a DAPT can also protect children's inheritance from their creditors.

Specifically, a trustee can make discretionary distributions to children so they can be provided for, but children's creditors cannot reach the assets still held in trust because the children do not actually own those assets. Children can also be protected from squandering assets, because they have no interest to sell, assign, or give away. For example, the trust could purchase a home for a child's rent-free use, but ownership of the home itself would be outside of the child's estate.

3. *Estate tax planning:* As a general rule, if someone establishes a trust, and the assets of that trust are subject to the claims of the settlor's creditors, then those assets are included in the settlor's estate for estate tax purposes. However, a properly drafted, funded, and operated DAPT can hold assets without those assets being subject to estate taxes at the death of the settlor because the assets of the DAPT are not subject to the creditors of the settlor or the beneficiaries.

4. *Establishment of a situs for the trust:* Unlike most states, states with DAPTs have identified specific requirements to qualify as a trust in that state. A trust can qualify as a DAPT as long as the trust meets minimum state requirements of the state allowing DAPTs. It's possible to set up a DAPT in a state even if the majority of assets are not in that state and even if some of the trustees are residents of states without DAPT statutes.

5. *Ability to generation-skip assets and avoid future estate taxes:* As discussed earlier, generation-skipping transfer taxes can apply if you attempt to transfer assets to generations that are more than one level removed from an individual. There is an exception that allows for a transfer of a certain amount of assets to individuals who are one or more generations removed from the individual transferor without such repetitive tax as each generational level. A properly operated DAPT uses this exception to generation-skip for a potential unlimited number of generations and thereby deprive the IRS from the opportunity to tax the assets at each generation.

In order for the assets of an irrevocable trust to be protected from the claims of a settlor's creditor, the transfer of assets to the trust must not be a fraudulent conveyance. Creditors generally have a limited period of time (usually two to four years) to challenge a transfer to a trust as a fraudulent conveyance. Pursuant to the Bankruptcy Code, the court may set aside any transfer made to a self-settled trust within ten years of a bankruptcy filing as a fraudulent conveyance if the settlor made such transfer with actual intent to hinder, delay, or defraud any entity to which the settlor was or became indebted.

Business Entities

Business entities can also be used not only to effectively and efficiently own and operate business activities but also to effectively compartmentalize risk. Think of assets as either hot assets or cold assets. Cold assets are those whose risk of loss is limited to the investment, like stock in publicly traded company. If you buy stock in ABC Inc., you may lose your entire investment if ABC goes bankrupt, but you're not otherwise liable for the debts and obligations of the company itself. The same is true for most bonds and mutual funds.

Hot assets, on the other hand, are those whose potential risks of loss could exceed the amount of the investment. Purchasing real property with a mortgage is an example. You may put a down payment of 10 or 20 percent, but if the underlying value of the property drops by more than your down payment, you could be liable for more than just your initial investment. Furthermore, if the real property being purchased is going to be a rental property, and someone is injured on the property due to a defect, the owner of the property could be personally responsible in a lawsuit resulting in damages being awarded that far exceed the equity you have in that property and even the overall value of the property itself.

Business entities can be used to cool down assets by compartmentalizing the risk associated with a particular venture by having the entity itself engage in the business activity or investment. They compartmentalize different and distinct business activities so that if something goes wrong in one business, others are less affected or not affected at all. Of course, to the extent you personally guarantee the debts and obligations of the business or otherwise assume the liabilities of the company, the protection can be lost.

Corporations: Business owners and investors have long used corporations as one of the most common business structures. A corporation is a separate business with a separate legal identity from its shareholders. Corporations have several important characteristics that are attractive to business owners and investors. Shareholders of a corporation enjoy limited liability, which means the shareholders are not personally subject to the debts and liabilities of the corporation and are not personally responsible for the corporation's activities. A corporation has centralized management where ownership through shareholders is distinct from the management operations provided by the management team or group customarily referred to as the board of directors. A corporation will typically also have officers who conduct the day-to-day operations of the corporation.

Limited Liability Companies: LLCs have numerous characteristics that make them attractive to small business owners and investors, the first of which is limited liability for all members. In a corporation, the investors are referred to as shareholders, who receive shares for their respective investment. In the LLC a contributing person becomes a member and typically receives units and/or a percentage of ownership in the LLC. The limited liability protection provided to LLC members allows both the passive investment members and those members taking an active role in the administration and management of the business to enjoy limited liability protection. The LLC member's liability is limited to his or her interest or investment in the company, although a member can be found personally liable in the event of any personal guarantee made by the member.

The LLC provides great flexibility for its members. State laws governing LLCs generally provide wide latitude for members to dictate the terms of operation and to reduce those terms to an operating agreement. In the absence of an operating agreement, state laws generally provide default rules for administration, but the members can often contract around or out of those default rules. This makes for large opportunities for various types of investors, whether passive, active, preferred, or a combination of investment options.

Captive Insurance Companies: A captive insurance company is a separate insurance company that can be set up to insure against risks that one or more operating companies could face, and which aren't generally insurable on the open market. Risks covered by a captive insurance company could include regulatory or law changes, loss of significant suppliers or buyers, intellectual property loss risk, and even the loss of key employees (there are dozens more risks that captives can legally insure against: data breaches, loss of key employees or customers, product warranties, recalls, copyright infringement, equipment breakdowns, regulatory changes, lawsuits – even cyber risk). Unlike most insurance companies that are publicly owned or owned as a mutual company, the business owner who is insured and/or his family can also own the captive insurance company and can benefit from the unused premiums if the risks do not materialize.

Conclusion

Reducing or even eliminating the three corrosive elements in the transfer of financial wealth can allow you to preserve more resources that can be used to pass on flint and kindling to a greater number of future generations. Try not to get caught up in, or overwhelmed, by the number and complexity of options. This summary is simply intended to allow you to compare your current tools with the stable of tools available to effectuate your Entrusted Planning.

QUESTIONS TO CONSIDER

1. What level of personal responsibility do you feel to reduce the erosive effects of division, taxes, and outside attacks on wealth transfer?

2. Do you see value in concentrating a portion of your assets and protecting them for multigenerational benefit? Why or why not?

3. Have you seen or experienced situations where assets were eroded because of one or more of these outside forces?

4. How much time did it take you to create your estate, and how much time have you put into protecting it?

Chapter 8

Discipline 7:
Entrusted Families Design and
Implement Dynamic Governance

"If your actions inspire others to dream more, learn more,
do more, and become more, you are a leader."
—John Quincy Adams

EACH YEAR, MORE THAN ONE million visitors wait in line
at the National Archives in Washington, DC for the chance
to see among other artifacts and treasures of American
History, what are generally recognized as the three most
important documents in the formation of the nation: the
Declaration of Independence, the United States Constitution, and the Bill of Rights. In fact, when History News
Network took a poll in 2013 of what Americans considered
to be their country's ten most important documents, they

specifically excluded these three documents because they would be the top three "practically by default."[1] These documents have collectively come to be known as the Charters of Freedom, and they have stood for more than two hundred years as the foundation for how the United States acts and operates.

The signing of the Declaration of Independence in 1776 is generally recognized as the event marking the birth of a new nation, and the ratification of the Constitution as the event that formally established self-government in the Colonies previously ruled by England. While the Declaration of Independence and the US Constitution are displayed side by side at the National Archives, they actually are quite different documents.

The Declaration was just that—a declaration that individuals have rights and liberties and the power of any government derives its "just powers from the consent of the governed." It is a document of *why*. The fifty-six delegates who signed the Declaration knew full well the potential cost of their fight for freedom when they concluded the Declaration with these final words: "And for the support of this Declaration, with a firm reliance on the protection of divine Providence, we mutually pledge to each other our Lives, our Fortunes, and our sacred Honor."

The US Constitution, on the other hand, contains little if any rhetoric, and the Preamble marks its only truly lofty

1 http://historynewsnetwork.org/article/150152

or aspirational language. In contrast to the Declaration, the Constitution is a document of *how*. It outlines the three branches of government and the separation of powers. It outlines how the States are to deal with each other and be, well, United. It also addresses how leaders are to be selected and replaced as well as how the Constitution is to be amended from time to time. Together with the Bill of Rights, these documents serve to create a structure within which otherwise autonomous states and individuals can effectively deal with each other.

Of the Family, by the Family, and for the Family

The transition from monarchical rule by a king or queen to self-government "of the people, by the people, and for the people"[2] was certainly not an easy one. The founding fathers had to try to balance the rights and freedoms of individuals with the need to have some form of governmental structure. They had to determine how power would be transitioned over time and how leaders would be selected and replaced. They also realized that whatever they established had to be flexible and amendable over time.

None of these, of course, were issues that were faced in a monarchy at that time. The king was in control, his determinations and decisions were beyond question, and his rightful heir would be his successor. Individuals were

---

2 From the *Gettysburg Address*, by Abraham Lincoln, November 19, 1863

subjects who had no particular rights or freedoms, or at least no rights that could not be taken away or altered by the king as he determined.

The issues that the founding fathers faced are actually quite similar to the ones confronting families, especially high-net-worth families, as they try to establish family governance to accomplish their goals, fully express their values, and use financial resources to effectively assist successive generations in fully realizing their own expression of "life, liberty, and the pursuit of happiness." Specifically, if a family wants to implement the disciplines outlined in this book for multiple generations, they must develop, cultivate, and perpetuate an organized family structure that captures, manages, and stewards both the family's human capital and financial resources. To do so, they must address the following questions:

1. How will family leaders be selected and replaced?
2. What parameters and guidelines will govern what can and can't be done with financial resources? In other words, how will the family's financial wealth be used to transfer flint and kindling to successive generations?
3. How will the structure balance the individuality and independence of each family member while still creating a supportive framework to accomplish the family's goals and objectives?
4. How will the structure allow for flexibility in the future without running the risk of having such significant changes made that it ends up running counter to the original intent?

The Exchange Zone

Any plan that involves more than merely dividing up assets and distributing them outright requires a system and process for effective governance. Although they may serve as benevolent kings or queens, the reality is that most high-net-worth families start out as monarchies. As long as the wealth creator is alive, they have the financial resources, control, and power. To effectively implement the disciplines outlined in this book, the monarchy must shepherd the family through a process to create and establish a representative family republic that holds and manages assets for the benefit of current and future generations. In order to accomplish this, the *founding fathers and mothers* must come to realize that the opposite of control is not chaos. The opposite of control is collaboration.

To be effective, governance must also be dynamic, a word that comes from the same Greek word *dynamos* as does the word *dynamite* (see Alfred Nobel case study). Dynamic governance is characterized by energy and effective action. It is a force that motivates, affects development, and creates stability.

In a four-person relay race, there are points at which each competitor races alone. There are also designated points in the race when two participants run together. These pivotal moments in a relay race take place in a spot called the exchange zone. As the first runner begins to approach the exchange zone, the second runner begins to slowly run.

The first runner enters into the exchange zone at full speed and continues to run. The second runner also runs in the exchange zone at full speed. At the handoff, the first runner passes the baton to the second runner.

Even at that point, however, both runners continue to run together, side by side. The runner passing the baton doesn't stop running until the handoff is complete. Without this process of running together and matching each other's speed and effort, time can be lost, the transition can be rough, and the baton may even be dropped. It is essential for the runner passing the baton to continue to run until the transfer has been successfully completed.

Family governance should look the same. Too often, the passing of the baton of financial control occurs at the attorney's office after the death of parents—much too late for proper mentoring or guidance. These transitions are often difficult: power struggles can be created among siblings, and family businesses can be thrown into chaos. It is during this period of time that we see the unfortunate transition in families from *we* to *me*.

By creating a family exchange zone, the passing of the baton from one generation to another can be a process that occurs over time while the wealth creators are still alive. A deliberate and thoughtful transition vastly improves the ultimate result and allows descendants to participate in family governance while also taking advantage of the wisdom and thought of the prior generation.

Options for Governing an Entrusted Estate Plan

Up to this point, we've talked about capturing the family's human capital, preparing descendants by providing flint (education and experience) and kindling (resources and opportunities), fostering and encouraging generosity, and preserving and protecting financial resources. Once you've addressed those issues, the last and potentially most important question becomes how to effectively manage and operate this new family enterprise now and into the future.

The reality is that there are as many governance options as there are families, each with slightly different advantages and potential issues. That said, there are some basic structures that families can start with and then fashion to achieve their particular goals and objectives. The key to any governance structure is addressing three things: *what* will be governed (structure), *how* will they act (governance), and *who* will serve (leadership).

Structure

By far the most common legal structure for holding assets on a multigenerational basis is the trust. In the prior chapter, we outlined the three-legged stool of a trust. *Trustees* manage the asset and make distributions from the trust to *beneficiaries* pursuant to the terms of the trust determined by the *settlors*. One of the key elements of a trust is that it can be the owner of the assets, so even as control changes over time, the owner-ship can stay the same. Trusts have been around for more than 800 years and have been used by countless families to hold and manage assets for beneficiaries.

To manage the taxes, protect the assets, and control the desires of the settlors, a trust typically needs to be set up as an irrevocable trust. That said, if it is going to effectively operate for an extended period of time, the trust must be flexible. As the world, laws, and tax policies change, a trust that will be in effect for generations must be able to adapt. One family we work with manages a trust established in the 1940s to provide educational benefits for successive generations. Because it was drafted nearly seventy years ago, it had a very limited definition of educational expenses and didn't contemplate expenses like computers, software, fees, or travel. To address the concern of establishing a long-term irrevocable trust structure with the need to have flexibility, two relatively new and powerful tools have been developed: trust protectors and decanting.

Trust Protectors

A trust protector is a person, group of people, or entity granted certain specific but limited rights to allow for greater accountability and flexibility. Some typical powers of a trust protector include removing and/or appointing trustees or committee members, modifying or amending the trust to adapt to changes in the law or to achieve more favorable tax treatment, adding or removing beneficiaries,[3] terminating

3 Through the use of special powers of appointment

all or a portion of the trust, and changing the situs (home state) of the trust. The trust protector typically has no power to invest, manage, or distribute the assets of the trust and cannot be a beneficiary of the trust.

The trust protector role can be especially useful during the initial exchange-zone period, when the parents are in the process of involving the next generation. The trust protector can be there to make updates or changes and serve as a protection for the parents in the event there are particular struggles or unforeseen issues during the transition.

Decanting

Decanting is the term generally used to describe the distribution of trust property from one trust to another trust pursuant to the trustee's discretionary authority to make distributions to, or for the benefit of, one or more beneficiaries. Named after the process of moving wine from one container to another, decanting can be used to either eliminate unwanted provisions in a current trust and/or add new benefits or provisions into a new trust.

Although decanting may be possible under common law, it is important for a trust to have express language authorizing a trustee to decant trust property to another trust. It is also critical to ensure that moving the assets of an existing trust into a new trust complies with applicable state law, that new beneficiaries are not added, and that the vested rights of existing beneficiaries are not impermissibly altered. The ability to decant can be limited so that it's only available during the life of the settlors (to prevent unwanted changes in the future) or can be structured so that a trust can only be decanted if the primary objectives of the settlor will still be achieved with the new trust.

Governance

Historically, a single trustee has been appointed to hold, manage, and invest the assets of the trust and to make distribution decisions pursuant to the terms of the trust. The laws of several states now allow the role of trustee to be divided into separate components.

Directed trusts are trusts in which some or all of the duties or responsibilities of a trustee are directed by one or more individuals or groups. A directed trust allows the settlors of the trust, often the parents, to divide the duties and responsibilities of a typical trustee into several different components. Directed trusts allow the settlors to continue to participate in *some* duties and responsibilities (like investment and management decisions) while removing them from the ability to make distribution or other decisions that might otherwise eliminate some or all of the asset protection and tax benefits typically associated with a trust.

Accordingly, trusts now may divide the role of trustee into one or more of the following types of trustees:

- *Investment trustees:* Investment trustees have the sole and absolute authority to execute documents or make and effectuate other decisions regarding assets of the

trust including, but not limited to, the purchase, retention, and sale of any assets held by the trust.

- *Distribution trustees:* Distributions trustees have the sole
and absolute authority to make and any discretion over
beneficial payments, distributions, uses, and accumula-
tions of income or principal to or for the benefit of the
beneficiaries pursuant to the terms of the trust.

- *General /administrative trustees:* General or administrative trustees have the sole and absolute authority to
exercise all powers conferred by applicable law to the
extent such powers have not been specifically granted
exclusively to the distributions or investment trustee.
Typically, the general or administrative trustees hold
title to assets and otherwise act at the direction of the
investment and distribution trustees.

- *Qualified person trustee*: The qualified person trustee
typically retains the powers and responsibilities necessary to properly situs the trust in a particular, desired
jurisdiction. This role is usually limited to only those
duties necessary to comply with the governing law, so
all other duties are vested in the other trustee(s).

This division of responsibilities among different individuals, groups, or entities takes advantage of certain skills,
abilities, or knowledge while still allowing other individuals
to participate in the management of the trust.

In states that recognize directed trusts, trustees are also
often relieved of liability to the extent that they follow the
direction of others appointed with those responsibilities.

In addition, the IRS has ruled that a properly drafted and operated trust can even allow the settlor of a trust to make certain investment decisions without affecting the potential estate tax benefits of the trust.

Directed trusts allow the family to divide the role of trustee into different functions and then fit the functions to the differing skillsets and passions of the children, as when there are a number of different business interests. If the trust assets consist of land, a sports or entertainment enterprise, and a manufacturing concern, the children who are interested in and experienced with one or two asset classes, but not the others, can be given a place on a committee that manages only those assets.

Leadership

The development and selection of family leadership is often the most critical issue when it comes to family governance. Four general options of the *who* exist: family counsels, family trustees and professional trustees working together, corporate trustees, and hybrids. These structures can operate either within a traditional structure (that is, where a board of trustees is appointed to oversee all of the trust operations) or in a directed trust structure (that is, where the role of trustee is divided into different components).

Family Counsels

Family counsels are structures in which the parents and/ or children self-govern the trust. In this structure, typically each eligible child over a certain age is given the right to serve as trustee or to appoint a trustee on his or her behalf. If there are three children, for example, the three children would serve together and upon the death or resignation of a child, his or her descendants would collectively vote to select a replacement so that there are always three trustees managing the assets for multiple generations pursuant to the terms of the trust.

The primary benefit of family counsels is that the people most invested in the outcome are the ones with the power to make decisions. The drawback is that the family counsel is the one charged, in essence, with imposing the parameters and restrictions established by the trust upon them—which can result in the fox guarding the henhouse. The current generation is the only stopgap to ensure the terms of the trust are followed and that the funds aren't used for other purposes, including benefiting current generations for purposes that fall outside of the scope and intent of the trust, rather than preserving the benefits of the trust for multiple generations. A concern may also exist that the children do not have the necessary skillsets to effectively manage the kind or level of assets. As a result, many families who use family counsels establish age, education, and/or experience requirements for a family member to serve as a family trustee.

Family Trustees and Professional Trustees

To counteract some of the issues of children serving alone, a board of trustees similar to a board of directors in a corporation could be structured to consist equally of both family trustees and professional trustees working together. The professional trustees would work side by side with the children to manage the trust.

Usually, the trust requires that the professional trustees are licensed certified public accountants, attorneys, or certified financial planners who are not related to the family. They are trusted professionals appointed to the board rather than hired for a specific purpose or function. They are truly trustees in the sense of the word with the attendant fiduciary duties.

The family trustees and professional trustees serve together with equal power. In the example of the family with three children of the current generation, the three children would serve as trustees along with three professional trustees for a total of six trustees. Any vote to take action would require four of six to agree. As a practical matter, the children would have to reach a consensus and convince at least one of the professionals of the prudence of the proposed action. It would also work in the reverse. Namely, if the professionals agree, they would still need to convince at least one of the children to vote with them. This system builds in check and balances in terms of control and adds a level of independent professionalism to the family trustees.

Corporate Trustees

A corporate trustee is a bank or trust company that performs the role of trustee. Corporate trustees can be advantageous because they are professional entities specifically organized and operated to act in a fiduciary capacity. They include trust officers, investment advisors, accountants, and financial professionals.

They also typically have structures and processes in place to oversee and manage distributions to beneficiaries pursuant to the terms of the trust. In essence, the corporate trustee brings together all of the skill sets and abilities necessary to effectively run a trust. When combined with the financial management of the assets, this can be a very cost effective option. Trust companies can also exist in perpetuity which can help with long term trusts. Although families are often concerned about the loss of control that can appear to occur when a corporate fiduciary is named, mechanisms can be put into place inside the trust that allow the family to remove a corporate trustee and replace that trustee with another corporate trustee. When corporate trustees can be removed, it can foster a greater sense of responsiveness and accountability on their part.

Hybrid Model

Families incorporating a hybrid model are looking to balance family involvement with outside professionalism and accountability. The hybrid model involves using a combination of family, professional, and corporate trustees to manage the trust. For example, the family may be placed in charge of family property, the family may jointly make investment decisions with professional trustees or a corporate entity, and a corporate entity may be solely responsible for distribution decisions.

Private Trust Companies

Many families have multiple trusts and may oversee charitable entities like private foundations or donor-advised funds. When multiple entities are involved, it can become difficult to replicate the right governance and appropriately integrate and coordinate different trusts with different objectives. You may also have family members or professionals who are reluctant to serve as trustees, because they are subject to the highest level of fiduciary responsibility that exists under the law.

A private trust company (PTC)—an entity engaged in business for the benefit of a single family (that is, an individual or married couple and his/her/their lineal descendants)—offers several unique advantages over the direct appointment of family members as trustees. First, PTCs offer limited liability for trustees because the PTC acts as the trustee and officers and directors of PTCs are subject to lower fiduciary duty standards than trustees of trusts and are more easily indemnified for their actions. They can often obtain directors and officers insurance, whereas trustees often find it difficult if not impossible to obtain appropriate insurance coverage.

Second, the business models of PTCs are more flexible than irrevocable instruments like trusts and can more easily adapt to changes. They can also establish various committees to manage specific assets or achieve specific objectives like a directed trust. Common PTC committees include distribution committees, investment committees, amendment committees, and committees that oversee, foster, and develop the human capital of the family through traditional and specialized education. A PTC can also be more easily amended and modified.

Third, PTCs can often serve as the trustee of a wide variety of entities, including dynasty trusts, charitable remainder trusts, private family foundations, and insurance trusts. This allows for more coordinated management of a family's holdings, especially on a multigenerational basis. PTCs can hold and manage the assets of multiple trusts (or sub trusts) and reduce costs or fees by collectively reaching higher breakpoints. A PTC can also be organized with a perpetual existence and can remain as trustee for the lifetime of the trust(s).

PTCs are not, however, without issues. Effective family coordination and decision-making may be challenging depending on family dynamics if the board of directors or shareholders is made up of a large number of family members. In such a case, some of the relationship issues that the family may have been intended to avoid by establishing a trust may arise again through shareholder squabbling. PTCs must be established in states that allow them, and most of those states have substantial capitalization requirements. The PTC must be carefully and deliberately organized, structured, and operated to avoid running into tripwires that can unravel the tax and asset protection benefits afforded to the trusts they manage.

U.S. Trust Company, Bessemer Trust, and Northern Trust are examples of companies that originally started as PTCs and then expanded their services to include individuals and families outside of the original.

The Family Office

Whether as part of a PTC or as a separate entity, many high-net-worth families elect to establish a family office to act as the operational nerve center of the family. Family offices became popular in the 1800s. In 1882, John D. Rockefeller established an office "of professionals to organize his complex business and financial operations and to manage his family's growing investment needs."[4]

Family offices are built and structured on a customized basis and it would be rare for two family offices to look and operate identically.[5] That said, family offices tend to have some things in common. They are usually corporations or limited liability companies staffed by family and non-family members and typically engage in one or more of the following activities as determined by the needs and preferences of the family:

- Managing the liquid assets of the family

---

4 http://www.rockco.com/our-history
5 As our good friend Scott Mathewson of Wellspring Associates says, "If you've seen one family office, you've seen one family office!"

- Overseeing the closely held assets of the family and appointing directors and officers to oversee those operations
- Coordinating accounting and legal services and ensuring that all necessary legal and tax requirements are met
- Capturing, preserving, and passing on the human capital of the family (as discussed in Chapter 2)
- Coordinating the traditional and nontraditional education of the family, including organizing and operating regular family retreats, conferences, and get-togethers
- Managing real property and legacy assets like vacation homes, personal property, ranch lands, and other unique holdings
- Providing concierge services like travel arrangements, household staffing needs, and family benefits
- Overseeing charitable activities, services, and support to assure they are impactful
- Coordinating distributions of family resources to family members pursuant to the terms and conditions laid out in the trusts and entities operated and managed by the family office.

In addition to the benefit of a centralized, professional and knowledgeable staff, family offices can be operated to create better communication in the family. Like any professional enterprise, the family office should make sure it has clearly identifiable goals and objectives and employs experienced outside professionals (attorneys, accountants, financial professionals, and family coaches) to achieve those objectives.

One of our favorite illustrations of the success of a family office can be told in the history of the Henry Phipps and the formation of Bessemer Trust Company. Henry Phipps was a partner with Andrew Carnegie in Carnegie Steel. In 1907, Mr. Phipps formed a family office known as Bessemer Trust Company. The name *Bessemer* refers to Sir Henry Bessemer, who is credited with revolutionizing steel manufacturing and was key to the success of Carnegie Steel. Bessemer Trust was created to manage and control the tremendous wealth that was generated through the sale of Carnegie Steel and the share of proceeds Mr. Phipps was to receive in this transaction. In 1911, Mr. Phipps wrote the following letter to his children (keep in mind these are 1911 dollars discussed):

My Dear Hal,

I have today transferred to your name two million dollars ($2,000,000) in bonds and two million dollars ($2,000,000) in stock of the Bessemer Investment Company, which I wish you to regard as a trust from me for the benefit of yourself and your children after you. It is my desire that neither the stock nor the bonds of the company shall pass out of my family and that you will agree among yourselves that the others shall have an opportunity to buy at a fair price the stock and bonds of any one before a different disposition can be made. I hope that the management of the affairs of the company shall meet with approval of each one, but should a difference of opinion arise, I desire that the judgment of a majority of you shall be controlling on all questions of policy. I advise that you approve action by the board of directors of the company in reserving all net profits as additions to surplus account and in declaring no dividend on the stock for at least ten years.

I urge upon you to live within your income and not to be a borrower on your own account or through the company. Realizing that changed conditions may arise which will require freedom in action to meet them, I have not fixed rigid limitations as to possession and control of this property but have indicated my earnest desire that a prudent and conservative management of the company shall be maintained and enforced and that each of you shall put proper restrictions upon your expenditures and lay aside a reasonable proportion of your income.

I have full confidence that this advice will be respected and followed by all of my children.

Your affectionate father,

Henry Phipps

Henry Phipps recognized that a centralized management company was critical to the success of this legacy. He recognized that each of his children might very well have their own ideas about how to use, enjoy, and deploy the financial wealth created, resulting in a diffusion of assets and the power of keeping the assets together for management purposes in preventing the depletion of the assets. Today, Bessemer Trust Company's largest clients are still the Phipps family members, and it manages more than $100 billion in assets.

In the Entrusted Planning process, each family will need to develop their own unique system of governance, developed through a very thoughtful process and crafted in such a way to recognize the multigenerational view of Entrusted Planning.

A Word of Caution

Approaching governance with the family can sometimes be a difficult endeavor that will require the family to work through issues of communication, expectations, and varying degrees of potential dysfunction. This may require professional assistance before meaningful dialogue can occur. Although many families successfully navigate the waters of the exchange zone, it's important to determine ahead of time what is and isn't negotiable. Whenever you sit down with your children or descendants to fashion a plan for the future, it's critical that you determine which issues are up for discussion and which are not. For example, if you want to ensure that leadership positions in the family require certain minimum educational or experience levels, don't open up these requirements for discussion. Descendants can become quickly frustrated if they think they have a say in matters when they actually don't or when they're asked for their opinion on matters that have already been decided.

In addition, governance should result in collaboration and not coercion. As mentioned at the beginning of the chapter, one of the hallmarks of the Declaration of Independence is that individuals should have the inherent right to pursue their own version of happiness. Many parents, with only the best of intentions, encourage their children down certain paths or to participate with the family during times and seasons when the children may not otherwise want to participate. Although there is nothing wrong with using your own assets as you choose, it's critical that you not seek to use financial resources to force descendants to engage with the family or its businesses. Allow family members to participate and be involved on such terms and conditions as they wish.

Finally, it's critical that you (and each succeeding generation) attempt, as best as humanly possible, to soberly judge the relative strengths and abilities of each family member. Before someone is assigned a role, carefully consider whether he or she has the skills, abilities, temperament, and personality to succeed in that endeavor. Being part of a family should entitle someone to certain rights and privileges, but that doesn't mean it should be presumed that they can or will succeed simply because of their last name.

One of the nastiest estate fights we've been involved in was a direct result of irrational emotions among family members taking priority over the health of the family. In this situation, a father had implemented a very standard estate plan. The father in this case had two children, a son and a daughter. He had equal love and affection for each of his children and therefore decided to name each as a fiduciary power holder in his planning, should he not be able to act himself. The father appointed his son as the executor of his estate under his last will and testament, and he named his daughter as the successor trustee of his revocable living trust.

The purpose of the will in this case was to catch any assets the father had not put into his trust during his lifetime and dump, or *pour over,* these assets into the trust at the time of his death. The trust was the vehicle the father used to actually dictate how assets were to be divided at his death. The father appointed each child a different position in order to give each a role to play, since he was concerned that although the daughter was clearly the better decision maker, the son would feel slighted if his dad did not appoint him to do something.

No one could foresee the health problem the father would face in his old age, causing his daughter to move in with him and take care of him for the remainder of his life, while the son did not assist at all. A strong animosity developed between the siblings, as the sister felt that she was doing all the work and that her brother had abandoned their father. By the time the father passed, the brother and sister despised each other.

When the brother refused to turn assets over to his sister (the trustee) as the last will and testament directed him to, she retained our firm to help her. We formally requested that the assets be turned over, but that request went unanswered, as did numerous other attempts at informal solutions. We wound up having to go to court and have a judge order the brother to turn the assets over to his sister.

The brother refused to follow the court order, citing his significant distrust of his sister as the reason for not turning assets over. When the brother continued to disobey the order, the court issued a bench warrant for his arrest. When the sheriff showed up at his door, his defiant stance quickly changed, assets were turned over, and the estate was ultimately finalized.

Out of his love and affection for his children, and his desire to placate them, the father unintentionally created a situation in which thousands of dollars in legal expenses could have been avoided. In determining family governance, choosing the person, people, and/or institution that will be the ongoing governing body is crucial. Personal fears of offending someone should never come into this process. You know your family. You know who makes good decisions and who does not. Keep the decision-making in the hands of those good decision makers. This may cause you to address some hard truths within your family, but do it now, or let your family figure it out in a court of law after you're gone.

Conclusion

Transitioning from a monarchy established by the wealth creator to a representative republic where every person in the family is valued and has a level of representation requires careful thought and a clear structure. Done well, the benefits of such a structure can continue well beyond the current generations and far into the future. It's the hallmark of Entrusted Planning.

QUESTIONS TO CONSIDER

1. How important is family leadership to you?

2. What are you doing today to prepare the next generation for their role in leadership? What still needs to be done?

3. Where are you in the exchange zone?

4. Who are the good decision makers in your family?

5. What qualifications do you think should be in place for your family members to participate in governance?

Chapter 9

The Entrusted Planning Process

An old man going a lone highway,
Came, at the evening cold and gray
To a chasm vast and deep and wide
Through which was flowing a sullen tide.
The old man crossed in the twilight dim,
The sullen stream had no fear for him;
But he turned when safe on the other side
And built a bridge to span the tide.

"Old man," said a fellow pilgrim near,
"You are wasting your strength with building here;
Your journey will end with the ending day,
You never again will pass this way;
You've crossed the chasm, deep and wide,
Why build this bridge at evening tide?"

The builder lifted his old gray head;
"Good friend, in the path I have come," he said,
"There followed after me today

159

A youth whose feet must pass this way.
This chasm that has been as naught to me
To that fair-haired youth may a pitfall be;
He, too, must cross in the twilight dim;
Good friend, I am building this bridge for him!"[1]
—"The Bridge Builder" by Will Allen Dromgoole

ON MAY 27, 1937, THE Golden Gate Bridge opened and instantly became the longest suspension bridge in the world. Stretching more than 4,200 feet long, with a height of nearly 750 feet, its six lanes support more than 110,000 cars a day, as well as countless pedestrians, bikers, and sightseers. The bridge connects San Francisco with Marin County and was named one of the Wonders of the Modern World by the American Society of Civil Engineers. It has become an icon of not just San Francisco but the entire State of California. It is generally considered to be the most visited and photographed bridge on Earth.

As with any massive project, the task of designing, approving and building the Golden Gate Bridge was not an easy one. Before work on the bridge could even begin, numerous obstacles had to be overcome. The Golden Gate Ferry Company operated ferries to connect the two sides and strenuously opposed the bridge because it would undermine

---

1 Source: *Father: An Anthology of Verse* (EP Dutton & Company, 1931)

their virtual monopoly. The US Navy was concerned that if the bridge was attacked or otherwise destroyed, it could negatively affect or even cut off access to San Francisco Bay from the Pacific Ocean. Local unions wanted to ensure that the project would hire only union workers. And finally, the effects of the Great Depression made financing the project overwhelmingly difficult.

Although all these issues made building the bridge difficult, it was the design of the bridge that perhaps caused the most concern and took the most effort. To be successful, the bridge had to be high enough to allow for naval shipping underneath. It had to withstand the constant effects of powerful ocean currents and salt air. Most dauntingly, it had to be longer than any other bridge of this type ever constructed.

To accomplish all of these objectives, the designers of the Golden Gate Bridge eventually settled on a suspension bridge model. A suspension bridge relies on two towers on each side. The towers are constructed first and then the road is slowly built out from each tower toward each other and also toward the two shores. Eventually, the two towers connect to each other and complete the overall connection of the two sides.

The Golden Gate Bridge took nearly twenty years to design and finance. Once construction started, it took just slightly more than four years to build at a cost of $35 million ($580 million in today's dollars). To maintain the bridge and keep it operational, two hundred workers continually paint, repair, and update the bridge. They're constantly replacing various parts of the bridge, including more than 1.2 million rivets that hold it together.

The Entrusted Planning Process

Bridges have been used throughout human history to connect locations and ease travel across otherwise difficult or insurmountable obstacles. The poem "The Bridge Builder," in which an experienced and successful person stops his journey to devote the time and effort necessary to create a structure that will make it easier for those who come after him, is a perfect example of the concepts laid out in this book. The builder did not simply carry the travelers across the bridge. Future travelers still had to make it to the bridge and walk across, but the builder gave to the future traveler a structure that would certainly assist them along that path and make their ongoing journey easier.

The process of transferring holistic wealth on a multi-generational basis is very similar to the process of building a suspension bridge. Both can be broken down into four separate and distinct stages: design, tower building, connection, and maintenance.

Stage One: Design and Align

Before beginning any substantial undertaking, it's critical to spend thoughtful and deliberate time and effort in the proper design so that you can effectively accomplish your objectives. Whether it's a bridge or an estate plan, you need to ask yourself some critical questions: What is my vision? What am I trying to accomplish? What load does the structure need to support? What is the topography and environment that I intend to build in? What obstacles or hindrances stand in the way?

As outlined in Chapter 2, the first stage in the Entrusted Planning process is to clearly identify and capture the human capital of the family. This includes identifying the family's core values, vision statement (or motto), and mission statement. Only when these have been identified can the blueprints for the bridge be developed. The importance of a well-thought-out and articulate family vision and mission statement cannot be overstated. They are essential for everything that comes after. These statements set the purpose and give direction to what the family is attempting to accomplish. In other words, how they want to get from here to there.

Many families find that hiring a personal family coach[2] to assist in this process is extremely beneficial. Without an independent, trained family coach to assist, families are left on their own to try to develop a plan and accomplish something that they have likely never done before. Experience is a key component to being effective and efficient in anything. Most families do not have any actual experience with how to bring these concepts together into one cohesive plan. It can also be difficult to step out of your roles as parents, children, and

---

2 Scott Mathewson refers to these people as "expert generalists", or people who know and understand the myriad areas that high net worth families must navigate.

grandchildren to create the kind of collaborative environment necessary during this stage.

In addition, mortality is not an easy or comfortable topic to address, and many are uncomfortable with the seemingly morbid topic of discussing what happens when mom and dad die. As a result, there may be an underlying uneasiness to the discussion. The use of a family coach should diminish this discomfort and switch the atmosphere from a discussion of estate planning to a discussion of the positive objective of creating a lasting legacy.

In addition to a family coach, it's also important to work with both an attorney and a financial advisor who understand and appreciate the concepts and disciplines outlined in this book. The attorney would be responsible for doing a comprehensive review of the parents' current legal documents, financial resources, closely held business interests, and unique or legacy assets. This review is critical so that specific legal or financial concerns can be properly identified and so that the family can ultimately determine whether or not the family's goals, values, and beliefs (that is, their intangible assets) are consistent with their estate planning (which would govern and direct their tangible assets). If they're not, they can decide what changes need to be made to properly align the two. A financial advisor would be critical in helping to ensure sufficient assets are available to meet the primary financial responsibilities outlined in Chapter 4 and to help determine where you stand on the inverted U curve.

Regardless of whether family members use a family coach, attorney, and financial advisor or work through the process themselves, this stage involves a lot of factual discovery. It has been said that once the facts are known, the issues present themselves. Once the issues are identified, then—and only then—can solutions be uncovered. Although this discovery process can take many forms, we've found that one of the best ways to ensure meaningful participation is to have a family retreat in which all members of the family meet and collaborate on the design process. Ideally, the steps to effectively use a retreat structure would include the following:

1. *Pre-retreat discovery:* This phase would involve the family coach interviewing the parents and doing certain personal assessments of each member of the family (that is, Myers-Briggs Type Indicator™, Strength Finder™, Communication Styles). The legal and financial team would use this time to gather all of the usual financial, legal and tax information.

2. *Family retreat:* The family would then participate in a one- or two-day event at an off-site location (that is, ideally not in their hometown). The event would start with identifying the family's core values, using a tool such as Rivets the Game™, reviewing the various assessments and developing the family's core values, vision/motto, and mission. The retreat should also include a discussion on the various personality types and communication styles so that family members would have better insight into how to effectively

understand and communicate with each other. Ideally, the retreat would be interspersed with recreational and team-building activities.

3. *Post-retreat follow-up:* To the extent it's necessary, the family coach should follow up with each family member post-retreat, looking for any potential dangers or risks the family may face (communication issues, trust issues, etc.), which may have come up during the discovery phase or on the retreat.

4. *Final blueprints:* The final step in this process would include finalizing the capture of all of the initial human capital as well as a detailed outline of how to implement the next three stages. There may be recommendations for specific outside help (that is, family counselors) with specific issues that need to be addressed. This would also be a forum in which the attorney presents his or her review of the legal and financial components and provides recommendations on how the legal structure could be properly aligned with the family's goals, values, and beliefs.

Stage Two: Tower Building

Like building a suspension bridge, once a design has been developed and finalized, the next stage would involve building two towers. The first tower is the parents' tower and the second tower is the children's and future generations' tower. Each tower is constructed at the same time, but separately and with one very common goal: to build the most solid and secure towers possible to provide the support to the entire structure and to ensure that the plan can handle the load it will ultimately carry.

The Parent Tower

A critical piece to the parents' tower involves capturing the narrative wisdom of the parents' lives. Our clients have fascinating stories to share about how they achieved their level of success. Often, they are rags-to-riches stories, and future generations need to know that the financial wealth did not simply appear out of the blue. What struggles were overcome? What successes and failures came along the way? What was the nature of the hard work necessary to persevere the wealth? This can be a very enjoyable experience since it requires only telling your story. Often a biographer and/ or videographer is employed to assist, and the final story can be produced as a book or video that can live on as an anthology for the family.

In addition to a biographer, many families hire a marketing team to help express their vision statement and mission statement in a visual way. The parents we work with are increasingly developing family logos, like family crests of the past, that allow them to visualize and express their core values and capture who they are as a family.

Once the mission statement, vision statement, and family anthology have been developed, the next step involves determining where the family sits on the inverted U curve, as outlined in Chapter 4. This means identifying where the family's wealth places them along the wealth continuum and determining the point at which the principle of diminishing marginal utility begins to apply (that is, where the negative effects of inherited wealth may come into play). Once that's established, the parents should determine how to redeploy any excess assets into flint and kindling (Chapter 5) and/ or generosity (Chapter 6).

With respect to flint and kindling, the parents will need to determine what behaviors they want to support and encourage, what opportunities they want to provide, and for how many potential future generations. Depending on the type and scope of the assets, this could be concentrated to something like education or could also include things like loans to start a business, funds for a first marriage, down payment assistance for a residence, or even assisting descendants so they can care for and raise minor children.

Parents will also need to determine the altruistic tendencies within the family. In other words, what is the family's plan for generosity? This has to be developed at the parents' level and then introduced to future generations. Younger generations may not understand the benefits of generosity and therefore be resistant to the idea of financial assets passing or flowing to someone other than them. As previously stated, a family's generosity will be personal to them and will necessarily take different forms and degrees. We have many families who are not charitably inclined at all and believe that their generosity is limited to their family. This is your plan and your advisors need to listen to you and your desires. If you're not charitably inclined, the idea of altruism should not be pushed on you. But the idea of generosity in such a case needs to turn into a discussion of how generous you're going to be within the family.

Although it may make sense to have discussions with the children and grandchildren regarding this analysis as you determine how to deploy any excess assets, at the end of the day it will be important that the parents be the ones casting a vision for their own wealth.

On the parents' side, stage two also involves identifying any issues the family as a whole or any individual member is actually facing that not only would impede the implementation of an Entrusted Plan but might also be so all-consuming that they overshadow a person's motivation to even think about these issues. It's essential that substance abuse, gambling problems, martial issues, ongoing legal troubles, health concerns, and mental issues be identified, professional assistance employed, and help obtained for those members of the family who need it. This should not stop the overall process from moving forward, and if there are members of the family with chronic issues that are not going to be solved any time soon, then that member's role (or lack thereof) in participating in the process needs to be determined. Troubled members of the family can always be plugged back into the process once they've appropriately addressed their personal issues.

Existing basic estate planning documents should be amended and restated to ensure that the planning aligns with the core principles, values, and objectives. This should be done—even if just as a temporary fix—to help align a family's vision and mission statement in a better way while the comprehensive development of your entrusted plan is taking place. The tools and strategies outlined in Chapter 7 should also be considered and implemented as appropriate.

One of the more difficult aspects of the Entrusted Planning process is the development of how the overall governance of the Entrusted Plan will take place. Obviously, the plan will be structured so that parents are in the decision-making seat for as long as possible. Once parents are no longer capable of policing the plan, who is going to take over the reins? Determining family governance can be difficult because irrational factors often creep into the decision-making process. As discussed in Chapter 8, not wanting to offend a family member by not putting them in a position of power, regardless of their inferior decision-making ability, have the potential to derail the entire process. During this stage, the parents should begin to develop very basic parameters for family governance. Although it's important for this to ultimately be a collaborative process with the children in stage three, the parents need to establish the rules of the road regarding what will and will not be negotiable.

The Children's Tower

As outlined in Chapter 3, at the same time the parents are building their tower, attention should also be focused on the construction of the children's tower, so that the two can ultimately be connected. Almost every aspect of the building of the children's tower is focused on life education and on leadership training and development. Fortunately, there are excellent materials and tools and even specialized companies that provide this type of training, with resources for children as young as five. Some life-education and leadership training is more general and focused on common principles and tools while other training can be specialized and focused on specific issues and the needs of particular families. Although it can be difficult, training and resources are also available for older and even adult children who may be showing the signs of entitlement or affluenza. This may take additional time and should be handled carefully, but such situations cannot be ignored if a successful bridge is ultimately going to be constructed and used.

Children are never too young to begin to be exposed to these concepts. In addition to outside assistance, we also encourage parents to include their children in discussions that are age appropriate. As the children get older, more intensive personal education can be implemented. We are often fortunate enough to meet with our clients' families, to meet their children, and even to have them sit in on meetings. We have also attended family retreats and shared about various legal topics to provide future generations with a head start on thinking about these issues. This also affords us the opportunity to meet the family and, more importantly, for the family to meet us. Too often the family is completely unprepared by not knowing who the advisors to the family are and whom to call in the event of death. Your family should know your advisors, and your advisors should be willing to make the investment in getting to know your family members.

Finally, building the children's tower is a good point to introduce the concept of generosity to them and to begin using the tools and resources outlined in Chapter 6. This is where you can give the children some resources and allow them to develop their own plans and strategies for being generous and engaged with the world. Allowing the children to speak to this component of your planning can not only help to engage them in the process but also will be a critical element to ultimately connecting the generations.

Stage Three: Connect and Implement

Stage three involves connecting the two towers and fully implementing the Entrusted Plan. The family story developed by the biographer and/or videographer is usually unveiled and time is given for each member of the family to reflect on the story as a whole and her part in it. The parents then outline the broad elements of their multigenerational plan for their wealth and the principles on which the governance plan, as outlined in Chapter 8, will be developed. A critical component of this stage will be to ensure that the children and successive generations know what to expect and what not to expect. The family's combined plan for generosity should also be finalized and implemented. The family coach, attorney, and financial advisor are often critical participants in this process.

There is no one-size-fits-all system for connecting the parents' tower with the children's tower. Within the parameters established by the parents, being open to letting the plan organically unfold is necessary to accomplishing the goals. It's so easy to lose motivation at this point. Everyone has put a lot of time into deep thinking and visualization of the future of the family, and the tendency to lapse back into apathy is overwhelming. This is especially true if the family has not previously contemplated this book's concepts. Put into place whatever measures your family needs to stay on course and complete the implementation. This is a great time to think of incentives in order to hold everyone's attention, like a wonderful family vacation upon completion.

Stage Four: Maintenance and Improvement

Just as in the process of bridge building, the work of maintaining the bridge should always be ongoing. After years of planning and construction, the Golden Gate Bridge stood in all its glory and splendor at its grand opening. Even though it accomplished its goal of connecting the two sides and it looked beautiful, crews almost immediately began the perpetual process of maintaining it. If they hadn't, the bridge would have begun to degrade within a short time and would ultimately fail. As with the bridge, constant maintenance of your Entrusted Plan is crucial.

At least once a year, we recommend that the family meet. The family vision and mission statements should be reviewed along with meaningful discussions about the family's individual and shared core values and principles. Our experience is that these will often change over time as a result of each family member's ongoing life experiences. Even if the mission and vision statements remain unchanged and the core values and principles are still applicable, the actual laws governing the plan may very well have substantially changed. For example, just since the year 2000, the laws affecting the federal estate tax have changed at least eight times. This doesn't take into account countless IRS regulations, tax court and other cases, and changes in trust and estate law that constantly affect planning.

Beyond simple maintenance, the Entrusted Plan should also be improved over time. As each family member proceeds down his own path of life, the entire family should regularly come together to share their experiences. Advisors can help maintain and improve the plan, since new planning techniques are developed every day and new laws adopted. These new techniques should be reviewed and potentially implemented to make the bridge stronger.

Improvement does not end at the plan level. Each member of the family should be encouraged to be consistently learning and pushing himself to improve. We have many clients who invite speakers and professionals from all walks of life to present at their annual family reunions.

One of our families recently became very interested in impact investing (as discussed in Chapter 6). This family had financial advisors well-versed in the concepts of impact investing attend their yearly family retreat in Jackson Hole, WY. Virtually the entire weekend was spent on the topic, with each family member being actively engaged in the discussion. As a result of this meeting, the family members completely redesigned their thoughts on philanthropy.

One of the members of the family was twelve years old. Although this twelve-year-old may not have been having as much fun as her friend out riding her bike for that weekend, imagine how much ahead of the curve this child is over her contemporaries in thinking about these topics. Unfortunately, this child's peers may never be required to think that deeply about the legacy being built in their own family.

No area of life should be overlooked in determining what your Entrusted Plan should look like. For example, we had a family bring in fitness and nutritional experts to speak. The family in question suffered from obesity and it had become obvious through the maintenance of their Entrusted Plan that the overall unhealthy lifestyle each member was living was negatively impacting the ability to accomplish the vision of the family. The family lost a combined two hundred pounds by the next year's family retreat, with two members finishing their first marathon. Health and fitness is now a very important core value for this family.

175

Conclusion

Each step in the Entrusted Planning process needs to be allowed to take its own course. Some steps may move very quickly and others may be painstakingly slow. Dedication to the process as a whole is critical and the only way to make sure that when a rough spot is uncovered, the family will persevere and overcome the obstacle, actually making the entire family unit closer. Although there is a clear step-by-step process for how Entrusted Planning should be implemented, each step in the path is its own animal that must be tamed.

Dedication and devotion to the process are critical for its success, and consistent review of the plan is necessary for its desired perpetual nature. Through the process of fact-finding, issue spotting, and developing solutions to the issues, each step—though daunting—is completed and the overall plan maintained and improved. The plan is fluid—it evolves as the family evolves.

The process should be viewed not as something that has to be done but as a system for the family to become closer than it has ever been. It's as serious an investment as any other made by the family. You have the opportunity to leave more than money to your family. You can leave a legacy.

We hope that if there is only one thing you take away from reading this book, it's that you're now empowered with the knowledge that your plan for your family does not need to look like everyone else's and that cookie-cutter estate plans most often are drafted to achieve exactly the opposite of what you would do during your life. Take control of your planning, demand more from your advisors and family, and cast a vision for your wealth that allows successive generations to fully engage with the world and continue a legacy of action, impact, productivity, and generosity.

QUESTIONS TO CONSIDER

1. Does your current estate plan tell anyone anything about who you really are and what your hope is for the future of your family?

2. What are you prepared to do to implement an Entrusted Plan?

3. What is currently preventing you from starting this tomorrow?

4. What part of Entrusted Planning rings true with you?

5. What is the biggest concept you take away after reading this book?

Putting It All Together: Robert and Ange Workman, A Case Study

Robert Workman—the Utah-based businessman who parlayed $250,000 Provo Craft and Novelty, Inc. into a tech-centered emporium valued at $250 million—and his wife Ange are among the growing ranks of highly successful individuals and families who are eschewing the traditional model of estate planning (that is, dump, divide, defer, and dissipate) and instead focusing on teaching their children that a life well lived is built on self-reliance and charitable giving. Their children know that they will not inherit the lion's share of their parents' wealth. Instead, they will have educational, entrepreneurial, and family-connection opportunities for themselves and their future generations. They will also have a hand in directing the distribution of family money to cultural and community-based development projects around the world. What they will not have, though, is a trust fund to underwrite a life of unearned ease.

Robert credits his parents and grandparents for a worldview that values making money and using it to repair the cracks in the world. He grew up in Lovell, WY, a farming community near the Montana border, influenced in large part by a no-nonsense grandfather. "He was an old rancher, tough as nails, and he taught me early in life that if something is broken, the means to fix it are within your reach," Workman says. Workman also acquired his grandfather's attitude of "STM": "Screw the Man." He explains, "I don't want people telling me it can't be done. It can be. We just have to figure out how."

The civic side of Workman's nature—the you-owe-the-world-something side—comes from his mother and grandmothers, Wyoming women attuned to the vagaries of climate and economics that are part of every farmer's life. One of Workman's earliest memories is of a neighbor sitting in front of his house eating bread and milk. "I asked him, 'Is that all you got to eat?' He said, 'Yeah, just bread and milk. I'm poor!'" Workman recalls that the man's poverty shocked him. "I ran home and told my mother, 'We've got to do something for him!'" No matter that the man was simply teasing a sensitive little boy. As Workman sees it, the die was cast: he had been trained since earliest childhood to lend a hand when a neighbor was in trouble.

Robert's parents got divorced around the time he started school. His mother remarried and stayed on in northern Wyoming. His father also remarried, later moved to Provo, UT, and in 1964 opened Provo Craft.

Before moving to Provo, Robert served a mission for the Church of Jesus Christ of Latter Day Saints (LDS). When his mission was over, Robert enrolled in Brigham Young University and worked part time in his father's store. His interaction with customers lent an added dimension to his business education. Robert experimented with their favorite products. And he got to know his customers as do-it-yourselfers, parents, churchgoers, gardeners, and hikers. On the product side, he learned about an arts and crafts cutting machine that, with a starting price of $3000, only high-income hobbyists could afford. He studied the available data about the crafts market and concluded that an affordable do-it-yourself (DIY) technology was an unmet consumer need.

"If we copied our competitors, Provo Craft and Novelty would be just another hobby shop," Robert says. "But if we pushed the limits of our dream, if we thought about crafts in a new way, we could change the marketplace."

As artists themselves, the Workmans knew they could design templates for a low-cost machine that cut vinyl, felt, fabric, and fondants (edible icing). Naysayers predicted that the product would fail. Who was going to pay $300 for a basic die-cutting machine? And how many crafters were out there anyway? Workman says he had the courage to move forward because he knew his market. Over the course of eighteen months, the Workmans, together with a creative team of designers, artists, and engineers, produced several iterations of a prototype they called Cricut.

Workman calls Cricut an overnight success. "My father had the wisdom of years behind him and ran a tight economic ship," he says. "And I had the vision that we could be a $10 millon-a-year company. He supported me as I pursued my dream."

The Workmans ran Provo Craft and Novelty together until 1984, when Workman senior retired. Robert bought his father out and stayed on as CEO. After twenty years at the helm, Robert felt an old desire to commit himself to the sort of community-development projects he had participated in as a missionary. To hone in on the right project, he drew up a list of human needs and came up with the following: portable power or electricity, shelter, food, and water.

With the list in mind, Robert, Ange, and several like-minded associates traveled to China, where Provo Craft and Novelty already had relationships with vendors and factories. To fund their first community-development project, the Workmans sold the company in 2005. They channeled most of the proceeds into Teaching Individuals and Families Independence through Enterprise (TIFIE), a humanitarian organization they founded. TIFIE's mission: fund self-sustaining enterprises in poor, dependent communities.

In China, Robert became acquainted with a citizen from the Democratic Republic of Congo named Phil. Phil had come to network with people and companies interested in establishing a profitable business in the DRC. He invited the Workmans to visit him there.

"Ange and I fell in love with the place and the people," Robert says. TIFIE began putting down roots in Congo. No need was greater in the capital city of Kinshasa than electricity. TIFIE's first grant funded the production of a small electrical grid intended to serve as the energy source for a range of small businesses. To Robert's consternation, though, business after business failed. Interestingly, the failures followed a pattern. While Robert was on site, business operations flourished. But as soon as local people assumed management, the money vanished. Eventually, Robert determined that employees were stealing from the company. Corruption was rife and it was undermining TIFIE's mission to lift a community out of poverty through entrepreneurship. "I was super-discouraged," Robert says. "I remember looking up at heaven and telling God, 'You can just take these people and shove it up their ass! They don't appreciate our work. I'm getting out of here.'"

But defeat was not an option. If Robert and TIFIE could not figure out how to establish an enduring enterprise in a poor, corrupt environment, who could? And if not now, when? He thought of personal heroes who undertook grand missions and confronted the pessimism and fear of their critics. Gandhi, Winston Churchill, and Ronald Reagan had not retreated in the face of routs and setbacks. Robert had to acknowledge that he and his organization were doing something wrong. "We simply didn't know how poverty drives corruption," Robert says.

He and his associates studied a specific case of corruption involving a trucking business they'd funded. The original plan had been to help farmers transport their crops from the countryside to Kinshasa. The business model involved cash transactions on the Kinshasa side. "How naïve could we be?" Robert says. "The truckers were skimming off huge quantities of cash."

Stolen cash was only half the problem. The Kinshasans would drive out to the farming villages and sell their tires to dump truck drivers they met along the way. Later in the day, the TIFIE trucks would roll back into Kinshasa on flat tires they took from the dump-truck drivers. Robert says he had never been exposed to such catch-as-catch-can thinking before.

"Generations of Congolese had operated in survivalist mode," Robert says. "That means when you have food, you eat it today because tomorrow it might not be there for you. A nongovernmental organization (NGO) like ours cannot just show up and say, 'Hey, guys, we're here to help you think strategically about the future.' The people we worked with were too poor to think about anything but the here and now."

Robert and his associates contemplated their core strength: they were inventors of useful products. Robert thought back to that list of basic human needs he and Phil talked about in China. In Congo, he began to think of those needs as four pillars. Without them, no community could expect to create a profitable business.

"It was my a-ha moment," Robert says. "We weren't going to change hundreds of years of cultural habits by imposing our strategic thinking on people. We had to be tactical. We would fund specific tools. We would teach individuals how to use them to create their own enterprises and their own wealth—one pillar at a time."

Robert and his team went back to the drawing board. They decided to move their operations from Kinshasa, the locus of government corruption, to Dumi, an outlying village. They established relationships with various tribal chiefs and together designed a five thousand-acre farm. Robert says the implementation succeeded because the chiefs believed themselves answerable to their people.

Although TIFIE continues to maintain several buildings and a communications center, the farm has been self-sustaining. Originally, a TIFIE seed multiplication project funded the cassava, pineapple, and sweet potato crops, as well as forty thousand hectares of moringa and acacia trees. In due time, the villagers themselves planted cassava, eggplant, hot peppers, and corn. Surplus crops are sold in local markets. Yearly income has increased from $30-$60 per family to $300-$600 per family. Along with greater economic stability have come a rainwater collection tank, a small school, and a health clinic. Solar panels, batteries, and lights have replaced kerosene lamps and candles.

Robert and his associates did good one pillar at a time. TIFIE's business model is sound because it insists that the community be part of the financial partnership. Rather than donate a $500 power system, for example, TIFIE charges the village $250 and makes up the difference with a matching grant. TIFIE does not dictate how the grid is used. Indeed, people in Congo and elsewhere with a vested interest in the utility infrastructure have chosen to establish different kinds of energy-dependent businesses, including roadside ice cream stands, cell phone charger stations, and schools.

"Instead of us running the show, we teach people how to use tools and then they figure out their own business plan," Robert says. "We ourselves had to learn that for a development project to succeed, the local people need to have skin in the game."

TIFIE has gone on to fund refrigeration, farming, education, and communications projects in many Congo villages.

The organization scrupulously avoids activities—notably mining—that invite corruption. "You can blame the mining corporations all you want, but the main problem lies in government corruption," Robert says. "Local politicians siphon off 50 to 80 percent of any contract."

Central to all TIFIE operations is the energy grid. Robert and his team created GoalZero, a developer of portable power products that first provided reliable, safe power and light for farms, water purification plants, brick-making foundries, and a mobile hair salon in Congo and Swaziland. The company name reflects Robert's philosophy that zero apathy, zero regrets, and zero boundaries lead to committed business solutions. Since the mid-2000s, GoalZero has made grants to dozens of small businesses around the world, including a surgical care program in Congo, a community police station in Ghana, a post-typhoon housing and school project in the Philippines, a solar installation in the Navajo Nation, and a portable smartphone charger project in New York and New Jersey after Hurricane Sandy.

GoalZero became so profitable that Robert sold it in late 2014 to NRG, a $14 billion energy company that supports clean, sustainable energy technologies. To this day, TIFIE partners with GoalZero and NRG on energy installations in Africa and Asia. Using the business model Robert hammered out in Congo, TIFIE worked with tribal chief King Nana Pra to build Kushea, a community technology center four hours outside of Accra, Ghana. Solar panels, batteries, tablets, computers, and Internet routers were purchased from GoalZero. TIFIE's Light a Village Program funded a solar backup system to run the center's fifty computers. King Nana Pra provided funding to train instructors. "Pretty darn cool that we could do something like that," Robert says.

TIFIE's community development work hinges on identifying the right partners. Robert says it took him ten years to develop a partnering paradigm based on well-defined business objectives and personal integrity. With dozens of successful business projects on the books, TIFIE and its partners now have the agility to SWAT-team themselves into disaster areas faster than most established NGOs.

For example, seventy-two hours after Hurricane Sandy knocked out power in New York and New Jersey, TIFIE and GoalZero were on the ground alongside Team Rubicon, a volunteer organization of military veterans who dive in as first responders. The 2012 joint effort relied on a fifty-three-foot trailer full of portable solar-powered equipment capable of recharging cell phones and powering critical life-saving equipment. "We still get thank you cards from the four thousand lives that our three organizations touched," Robert says. "We had the product, the willpower, the teamwork, and the money to get the job done."

Robert reenacted the drill after the April 2015 earthquake in Nepal. Seventy-two hours after disaster struck, TIFIE worked alongside other NGOs to set up a power source and twenty-four maternity clinics. Whereas the Hurricane Sandy relief project was a *one-and-done* deal, TIFIE expects to stay on in Nepal's Dhading and Sindhupalchok regions, where it will aid some 126,000 pregnant women left homeless by the earthquake and its aftermath. One of TIFIE's chief partners in Nepal is Barebones, another Robert enterprise that facilitates off-the-grid living and disaster relief with product lines such as tents, camping equipment, gardening tools, solar generators, and lights.

Unlike administration-heavy non-profits, TIFIE and Barebones stay afloat thanks to a small staff and a network of volunteers. One hundred percent of donations go toward development projects. An endowment, enriched through Robert's various businesses, funds projects and office overhead.

Robert points to his childhood in Lovell, Wyoming, as the foundation of his philanthropic ethic. Yet, he concedes that his humanitarian mission would not exist without a moral framework he calls the Four Ones:

1. *One with one*—your relationship with a higher power
2. *One with me*—your relationship with yourself
3. *One with you*—your relationship with another individual

4. One with community—your relationship with three people or more

Robert further pairs each of the Four Ones with three concepts: intention, respect, and choice. For example: What is your intention in having a relationship with a higher power? What is the nature of your respect toward that being? Based on your understanding of a higher power, what choices are you making in your life?

The Four Ones underscore the Workmans' belief that giving back is the ultimate expression of a successful life. Robert defines "successful" as doing good to get good. Indeed, humanitarian action is the legacy the Workmans want to leave their children and grandchildren. To that end, they have earmarked 5 percent of the family wealth for their eight children who range in age from twenty-one to thirty-eight and have established a fund to provide multi-generational educational opportunities, leaving the rest to go to charities and foundations. The children will rotate in and out as TIFIE board members. Each one gets a crack at spending the money on worthwhile sustainable projects.

In the final analysis, Robert and Ange Workman have tried to raise their children to believe as they do: that people out in the world—in Congo, Swaziland, Sierra Leone, Liberia, Nepal, Guatemala, Peru, Morocco—need the Workmans, and the Workmans need the people of the world as well.

Afterword

Things I Learned from My Parents and Hope to Pass On to My Children

by

David R. York

MY DAD WAS BORN IN a farm house in Auburn, KY and grew up in various small towns throughout the South, following his father, who worked long hours for small wages in dirty and dangerous sawmills. Eventually settling in Bowling Green, KY, my grandfather instilled in my dad the critical importance of education as a means of avoiding demanding physical labor and a life spent living paycheck to paycheck. My mom, on the other hand, grew up in a middle class family, bouncing back and forth between California and Florida, following her father, an aeronautical engineer working in the space program.

In many ways, my parents are clearly opposites. My mom loves English history and my dad likes war movies.[1] Mom was a voracious reader as I grew up, whereas I don't ever remember seeing my dad even open a book if it wasn't related to work. On one family trip, my mom took me to various historical sites, while my dad took my younger brother miniature golfing.

Despite their differences, they did and still do have many things in common. Both are smart, hardworking, and driven. Together, they built a thriving CPA firm from scratch. When each of my parents turned seventy years old, my brother and I presented them with a list of things we had learned from each of them. Although I didn't necessarily appreciate all that I had been taught at the time, as I reflected on each of their lives, I realized how much of what I do and how I tick goes back to things they instilled in me.

Things We Learned from Our Dad and Hope to Pass On to Our Children

1. The Value of Hard Work

Whether it was encouraging us to always do our best and the value of excellence or the constant reminders of the tough life of a ditchdigger,[2] our dad always encouraged us to

---

1 My understanding is that the only movie they were both equally excited to see over the course of their entire marriage was the move *Paint Your Wagon*, with Clint Eastwood, but that was only because my dad didn't know it was a musical.

2 Neither by brother nor I was a great student growing up. During the

work hard. He also modeled that word "work" in building an incredibly successful accounting practice from scratch. We learned that if we were going to do something, we should do it well.

2. A Commitment to Family

One thing we could always say about our dad was that he was committed to us, to the family, and to the best for us. He always wanted us to have it better that he did. He also made sure that we were in church every Sunday and heard the Word of God.

3. The Value of Education

Education was always emphasized as the key to choice in our lives. We were always encouraged to learn, to strive, and to advance, both personally and professionally. Not only did our dad encourage education; he practiced what he preached. He's a man who is always learning, studying, and pushing himself.

4. A Love of Country

Every day in the summer, Dad would walk down with us to a flagpole located near his office and proudly raise and

---

course of many long and drawn out discussions over our report cards, one of my dad's most common refrains was that if we didn't get better grades, we would grow up to be *ditchdiggers*. This always perplexed us because we had never in our lives actually seen anyone dig a ditch; nor could we figure out why someone would want or need to dig one. I came to believe that the term "ditchdigger" was a general reference to hard, manual labor.

lower the American flag, at least until he could get a flagpole of his own. We learned how to preciously and respectfully fold, honor, and care for the flag. Through his nearly thirty years of service to the US Navy and the pride he showed in our country, we learned that the United States was and is the greatest country in the world.

5. *How to Treat Clients*

He also taught us to work to make our clients successful, to hire them for our needs, and to refer others to them. Always take care of your clients. Their problems need your solutions. Work tirelessly for them. That's why he has had many of the same loyal clients for more than forty years.

6. *Never Give Up*

When faced with a problem or an issue, Dad taught us never to give up. Dad wouldn't stop thinking, working, or researching a problem for a client until he came up with a solution. Figure out a way to get it done. If you're diligent and tireless, you can solve most problems that come your way.

7. *Life Has No Sidelines*

Dad is a great example of always striving and making the most of he opportunities we have and the resources we've been given. Most people coast by in life so they can coast by in retirement. Not our dad. He still works harder than most people half his age. He still wants to push himself and learn and grow.

8. *You Can Learn Something from Everybody*

Dad taught us the value of conversation and of being interested in other people and what they did. He taught us that every person, even a ditchdigger, has something to share and something you can learn from them, whether it's a character trait or a piece of knowledge.

Things We Learned from Our Mom and Hope to Pass on to Our Children

1. *A Love of Strategy*

We learned at a young age to love baseball, but not just for the joy of hitting, fielding, and running the bases. We learned to love baseball because of the strategy and thought that go into each play. We also learned how to play card games that require strategy, and we were encouraged to not only think about our current move but the next three moves as well.

2. *Leadership*

As a working woman in a man's world, our mom had to learn how to command respect from her peers and employees. She taught us how to listen to others' ideas and then improve them to better the team as a whole. She taught us to step up and make sure things get done.

3. *Competition*

Whether it was in school, playing sports, or being a friend, Mom always wanted us to do and give our best. Growing up, we were never taught to do anything other than the best we could do—and sometimes more. She taught us to play fairly but to always play hard and to play to win. It was the best and only way to show you respected yourself, your competitor, and the game. Whether it was a game of cards or Air/Sea Battle on Atari, we were proud to beat our mom because we knew we always got her best.

4. Creativity

We were taught how to look at things differently. If we had a problem to solve, we knew that Mom would help us to look at all the possibilities and figure out which worked best. She realized that true creativity consists of seeing what everyone else has seen but thinking what no one else has thought. Her creativity can be seen in her pictures, the marketing and promotion of the firm, and in the look and feel of the office.

5. Loyalty

Stand by your man. Work hard for your company. Take care of your clients. Be loyal to your friends and family. From our first T-ball game until our last game of high school baseball, we knew that for each game we played in (or watched from the bench) that there would be one thing that was consistent—and that was our mom in the stands, with a scorebook in hand, watching us and cheering us on (even if she wouldn't give us a hit on a questionable error in the field).

6. Organization

If you're going to make a move, make a plan. If you're starting a business, make a plan. If you're going to buy groceries at the store, make a plan. Spend some time and effort thinking about what you're going to do and you'll be much better prepared and have a much better result.

7. Critical Thinking

Many people just accept what they hear at face value, without offering any critical thought at all. Not our mom. She taught us how to think about what others were saying or problems we were facing.

8. Excellence

If you're going to do something, do it well. Mom went through countless red pens to make sure our term papers, assignments, and even client letters looked and sounded professional.

Afterword

A Lifetime of Entrusted Planning

by

Andrew L. Howell

I WAS BORN A TRUSTIFARIAN. Yes, I am one of the potential heirs we are discussing in this book. My grandfather, Max B. Lewis was born in Rexburg, ID in 1918 to Jack and Hannah Lewis. My great-grandfather Jack Lewis was a Jewish immigrant from Latvia who settled in Rexburg. His primary occupation, among many, was trading in animal pelts. He was not financially wealthy by any definition. He was a very hard worker and always provided for his family and instilled an amazing work ethic in his three sons, all of whom enjoyed great personal successes in their own lives. Sadly, all have since passed away.

Childhood for my grandfather — affectionately called "Papa" by our family was not an easy one. Having Jewish heritage in a predominantly LDS community in the 1920s, his family was not necessarily welcomed into the neighborhood. Being financially poor, and not necessarily in the friendliest of networking environments, Max wanted more.

Max was extremely intelligent, good looking, and hard-working, but he also loved to have fun. An avid fly-fisherman, he loved the western rivers where he could chase rainbow trout while wading straight up the middle of the Henry's Fork's Box Canyon, a river he fished his entire life. I was three years old when he had me in oversized waders casting to fish I had no hopes of landing in that same river. That was Papa: actively involved in our lives and a firm believer of hands-on learning.

After graduating from high school, Max enrolled at the University of Utah and was very active in numerous organizations. He won a national level title in debate, which is understandable as I never won an argument with the man and never saw anyone else win one either. After graduating top in his class, he applied and was accepted to Harvard Law School, where he completed one year of studies before joining up for military service.

He was stationed in the South with the Air Force. One day, his commanding office gathered all the troops together and asked one simple question, "Does anyone in here have legal training?" Having only completed one of his three years at Harvard, Papa slowly raised his hand and indicated that he had one year at Harvard Law. Apparently, that was enough for the commanding officer, and he was whisked away, being put into the position of Judge Advocate General over seven bases in the southern United States. In the course of his remaining service, he tried more than four hundred military cases without ever having graduated law school. Seems unfathomable today.

After his service and discharge from the military, Max returned and finished his studies at Harvard. He told me that upon graduation, he finally felt free and decided to take a position with a very prestigious firm in California. After moving there, however, he felt discontent that he couldn't have a life outside of the office. He ended up moving again, this time to Salt Lake City, to continue practicing, but where he would have access to the streams and rivers he so clearly loved. For the next fifty-three years, he practiced law at a level very few attorneys ever achieve, and also went fly fishing.

He practiced exclusively in the areas of tax and estate planning, with a clientele that would make any estate attorney envious. From his office in Salt Lake, he represented families across the country that everyone reading this book would recognize. And he did it well. He assisted with very high-level planning—and was never sued once in his entire career. He never even had a client in an audit before the IRS and he was very proud of this fact. He was a keynote speaker around the country and trained many of today's elite estate planners and insurance agents. I have heard him called "The Dean of Estate Planning" by very influential players in the planning world. To this day, people still know about his legacy.

His death left a hole in my heart that I have never been able to fill. I had thirty wonderful years with this man, who was a behemoth in my life. His arm was always around my shoulder to help guide me on my path. I never realized how lucky I was until I started practicing on my own and met families who operated differently than we did.

As a byproduct of his hard work, Max was also financially successful throughout his professional life. He simply loved work and, as a result, enjoyed success in his work. Yes, despite being a four-letter word, "work" is not a bad thing. He taught me the love of being productive. Max never formerly retired; he thought it was the quickest way to becoming irrelevant.

From a very early age—I can't even remember how young—my sister and I were always included in family financial meetings. Monthly, or at least quarterly, the family would meet with our financial planners and accountant to discuss family finances. Max watched all aspects of the family like a hawk. Without his knowing it, and through his example, he was teaching us all how to play in the real world and talk with advisors.

At the meetings we were always told to be quiet and just watch, although we were welcomed and encouraged to ask questions. In the hundreds of meetings I attended by the time I was eighteen, I had picked up the vernacular of how planners talk. At eleven years old, I knew what a defective grantor trust was.

Max did not believe in hiding the ball. He wanted us all to know and be aware of what resources the family had, the opportunity it provided and the value it represented. He wanted us prepared to receive it. My entire childhood was so permeated with this other form of education that I simply assumed everyone else was getting it too.

I watched him put members of my family back in line, should they step out of our family philosophies. Most of the time, I was the one who needed correcting. We would work for him in the summers, and I remember one time being down at his office. I must have been thirteen or fourteen at the time and as arrogant a fourteen-year-old as you could ever meet. I was talking to someone in the hallway and making a stupid teenager statement to the effect that we were rich.

My grandfather never laid a hand on me. His stare of disappointment was always more powerful than any swat on the butt. That stare could make me wet my pants. However, this time Max heard my arrogant and entitled comment and all I felt was his massive hand on the back of my collar (he was 6'2" and very strong). He lifted me up, carried me to his office, slammed the door, and pointed his finger directly in my face and said, "Listen to me very carefully, I am rich. You don't have shit." He was ashamed of me. I had never experienced this reaction from him—ever. I knew with all certainty that I never wanted to experience it again.

Hours spent with him on a trout river with him having to untangle my line or losing an entire box of his two-dollar flies as it dropped in the river and floated away, never bothered him an ounce. He was patient, understanding and nurturing. But to him, working so hard to create what he had, only to have his spoiled, flippant grandson stupidly make such an entitled statement was too much for him and he cracked. He would not tolerate it, and he let me know that immediately.

This interchange is burned into my memory. It made me think about life much differently, of course after changing my underwear. To this day, the words "entitled" or "entitlement" immediately take me back to that experience and are significant trigger words for me. My grandfather has been gone for almost ten years now, and even at the age of forty, I think about that experience almost every day. It grounds me. Words of our ancestors stay with us.

Knowledge used to flow through the telling of stories and experiences. Book learning is relatively new to this planet. I can't remember one thing from my eleventh-grade Western Civilization class, other than that I despised the teacher and still do. I hope you read this book (you know who you are) and feel horrible that you didn't let me into AP English. But this moment in time with my grandfather that took less than two minutes is burned in my brain forever. It shaped my life and my work ethic and continues to do so to this day.

I certainly didn't know it at the time, but my grandfather was practicing Entrusted Planning throughout my entire life. I was brought up this way. It made sense to me and this is why I was so shocked when I got out of law school and began practicing in the field of estate planning. Other than my grandfather, the vast majority of my family members are lawyers, and I had a number of opportunities to work with them. However, I was very concerned with issues of nepotism, as my grandfather was well-known in this area. I avoided working with family altogether.

I became actively involved in the estate planning section of the Utah State Bar, and I got my own name out there. To be honest, I was rather shocked by how most estate planners practiced law. It felt very much like what we call in our book a "trust mill." There was a set process that all clients were run through, a production of documents and periodic, but sporadic review meetings. All emphasis regarding planning was "avoiding estate taxes" and passing on as much money as possible. There was very little, if any, time devoted to actually knowing the family that was being represented. It was foreign to me, and as a result, I refused to play this game.

My entire career I have attempted to impress upon my clients that they have an incredible opportunity to pass more of who they really are on to future generations. I have encouraged an open dialogue about finances in the home and have routinely met with families to speak with them about higher-level thoughts of passing on human capital. This was already part of my practice—the part of my practice I loved most. You could really see people begin to contemplate how they could make a more lasting impact with their wealth. It is fascinating to be in a meeting with a client who has never contemplated these issues before, and you get to see the wheels in their head start turning. It's as if they are hearing a cure to their ailments and concerns about their family for the first time.

My grandfather did an incredible job of building the bridge for my family to be empowered to receive wealth. Although losing him in 2006 was traumatic from an emotional standpoint, I deeply admire that from a legal standpoint, his affairs were completely in order. We as a family knew the advisors that had helped him—not just knew them but also had our own personal relationship with them. We knew who to call if something were to happen and we needed advice. We knew what was important to us as a family and how we wanted to use our financial resources to perpetuate the legacy he had created.

Before his passing, Papa wrote a book about his life, though we were not aware he was doing it at the time. It has become a treasured family heirloom. My grandfather's legacy has been my family's North Star. When making a decision, we often find ourselves asking, "What would Papa do?" Nine times out of ten we all wind up agreeing with each other on the outcome of this question. He spent so much time educating all of us. We knew him, and we knew our family.

When I met David R. York in 2007 and we began talking about issues related to our practice area and where we each saw it heading, we came to the conclusion that we both see a fundamental shift in how these upcoming generations view wealth transfer. We concluded that any planner would be remiss in not discussing these issues with their clients.

We have also witnessed a significant difference in how each generation is learning from each other now as opposed to the past. Unfortunately, the level of family education has dramatically declined. Schools, friends and, God forbid, the Internet are the education of upcoming generations. People have stepped away from the responsibility of educating future generations. They expect teachers at formal institutions to take on this responsibility. This is simply expecting too much of a teacher. Moreover, it is setting up future generations to lose sight of the uniqueness of their own family. I want my children's teachers to educate them in reading, writing, and arithmetic. I do not want the teachers to school my children on philosophies related to finances, wealth in general, or their own place in the family unit.

I do not care about the size of someone's estate. Entrusted Planning can be implemented to any level or degree. It's ultimately a mindset that asks you not to think of your *value* as strictly tied to the numbers in a bank account. It is being actively and meaningfully engaged with the people most important to you and assisting them across the bridge. It's using all your resources (not just financial) to perpetuate what has been important to you while you were on this earth and to ask how that human capital can live beyond you.

I love what I do because I love what I sell: the ability for someone to go home at night, crawl into bed, and fall fast asleep knowing that their affairs are in order and their legacy will live on. That is a comfort level that very few people can say they have achieved.

Continued Author Bios

DAVID R. YORK is an attorney, certified public accountant and managing partner at York Howell & Guymon. David received a B.S. from the David Eccles School of Business at the University of Utah and a J.D. from the S. J. Quinney College of Law at the University of Utah. He is a Fellow with the *American College of Trust and Estate Counsel* (ACTEC). David has been regularly named to Utah Business Magazine's Utah Legal Elite™ in the field of estate planning. He has spoken to numerous groups including the Hawaii Tax Institute, the Salt Lake Estate Planning Counsel, the Utah Planned Giving Roundtable, and TedXSaltLakeCity in 2015. He is actively involved in charitable activities with the Sunshine Heroes Foundation and Holding Out HELP, an organization that assists individuals and families transitioning out of polygamist communities. In his spare time, David enjoys cycling and photography. He lives in Cottonwood Heights, Utah with his wife Mindy and their five children.

ANDREW L. HOWELL is an attorney and managing partner at York Howell & Guymon. A Utah native, Andrew earned a B.S. degree from the University of Utah and his J.D. from the S. J. Quinney College of Law at the University of Utah. He is currently a member of the Utah State Bar, Idaho State Bar, Arizona State Bar, Texas State Bar and the Wyoming State Bar. Andrew was recognized in the Utah Business Magazine as one of the Utah's 2015 Forty under 40 and also recognized as Utah Legal Elite for the past 6 years straight. He has also been acknowledged as a Rising Star in Estate Planning by the Mountain States Super Lawyers List for the years 2010 and 2015. Andrew currently serves as the Chairman of the Estate Planning Section of the Utah State Bar and has served on that executive committee for the past 4 years. Andrew is rated "AV Preeminent" by Martindale-Hubbell, which is the highest rating awarded to attorneys for professional competence and ethics. Andrew is actively involved in the charitable and non-profit community having served on a number of boards and participating in the much needed "Wills for Heroes" program. While absolutely dedicated to and in love with his professional practice, Andrew spends his free time in the outdoors with a passion for fly fishing, archery hunting and skiing. He lives in Salt Lake City, Utah with his beautiful wife Candice and their three children.

Acknowledgments

From David R. York

To my wife Mindy. You are, far above all, the person on this Earth whom I admire the most. I am humbled and overwhelmed to have you as my best friend. You are smarter, stronger, wiser, and more loving than I could ever hope to be. You are the reason for the advice I give prospective grooms: Marry up and be grateful!

To my children, Emma (Strength and Charm), John (Thoughtful and Devoted), Samuel (Wise and Determined), Hudson (Passionate and Powerful), and Avery (Wonderful and Wild). You each amaze me. As you go forth in life, all I ask is this: Love God, love others, and press on!

To my parents, for teaching a less than perfect kid some pretty perfect lessons. Apparently I was listening, though even I didn't know it at the time.

To my brother, Michael, thanks for coming along and giving me someone to hassle, play with, be encouraged by, and love. You are an absolutely amazing person and I'm so proud to call you my bro. To Crystal, Caroline, Elizabeth (my birthday buddy!), and Victoria. What wonderful women to call my family!

To Andrew Howell, for daring to dream and being willing to not only take a leap of faith but for putting up with me and my occasional random thoughts and ideas.

To Paxton Guymon, for being willing to join us and bring such excellence, enthusiasm, and fun.

To Lee Brower, for starting me on this journey and helping open my eyes to the pitfalls and problems with traditional estate planning. Keeping seeing what everyone else sees and thinking what no one else has thought.

To Lee McCullough and Teresa Robison, for giving me a chance and taking me under your wings. I am appreciative beyond words.

To Bethann Finley and Alisha Scow. Thank you for your tireless work, effort, and excellence. Without you both, I would not be anything close to what I am today. Thank you beyond measure for putting up with me.

To all those who helped us put this book together, especially Robert Workman, Greg Spencer, Bill Townsend, Scott Mathewson, and Sara Stratton. Your insights and willingness to share are so appreciated.

Acknowledgments

From Andrew L. Howell

To my wife, Candice and my children, Thomas, Harrison and Madeline; this book is written for you. We are building the bridge together. Candice, thank you for showing me what is truly important in life and bringing three beautiful souls into this world. Thank you for your love, understanding and patience, which I know gets tested often.

To my Papa; You gave me my love of the law, of problem solving, fly fishing, Idaho, Montana and all that the outdoors have to offer. You taught me humility, how to be a gentleman, and how the luckiest time in business is found at 4:00 a.m. working at your desk. You kept me on the right path when I clearly could have taken another route. Unfortunately, you also most likely taught me my sense of humor and it saddens me every day to think I will not hear that amazing rolling belly laugh of yours. You were in my mind as every word was written in this book.

To my mother, Karen Freed who raised me with every opportunity that a child could ask for. You have taught me love, compassion, empathy and created my deep sense of loyalty to family. Our morning talks are one of the highlights of my day.

To my sisters, Angie thank you for being my partner in crime growing up and for making the family meetings we were forced to attend enjoyable with our inside jokes. When not fighting, we always seem to be laughing. Samantha, please read this book and absorb what it can mean for your life. Your intellect is amazing and your beauty matches. Your potential is there to do whatever you want. I love you both very much.

To my father, Robert Howell; you taught me to debate. To think critically and challenge common perceived notions. I owe my skeptical eye to you and it has served me very well.

To my law partner and Co-Author, David York; I am so grateful that when I came to you and said we should write a book in our "free time" you didn't laugh me out of your office. Your knowledge is second to none, your professionalism is an example and your drive to succeed is a testament. Our friendship is something I hold sacred.

To my dear friend, who also happens to be my paralegal; Erica Anderson; for the past seven years you have been by my side through all my crazy moves. You are incredible and I treasure you as a major asset not just to my practice, but my life as a whole.

Writing a book sounded a lot easier a year ago. We could not have done this without impeccable mentors, editors, proofreaders, and our amazing clients and colleagues willing to read it and give us feedback. You all have my deepest gratitude.